EMENT

BASICS

Sport Management: The Basics is an engaging and accessible introduction to sport management which considers a range of contemporary philosophical, social, cultural and political matters as they impact on this growing field. Drawing links between academic theory and practice, it explores the current challenges facing managers in the sport industry, addressing topics including:

- the history of sport management;
- the role of the manager;
- levels of management;
- the public, private and voluntary sectors;
- sport management in the global marketplace.

With many examples of how the concepts discussed relate to actual jobs in sport management, a comprehensive chapter on employability, and case studies which explore both theory and practice, *Sport Management: The Basics* offers a clear and concise introduction for anyone seeking to study or work in sport management.

Rob Wilson is Principal Lecturer in Sport Business Management at Sheffield Hallam University, UK. He has delivered sport management related courses since 2002, is the author of *Managing Sport Finance*, the co-author of *Finance for Sport and Leisure Managers: An Introduction* and has published a number of chapters in sport management textbooks.

Mark Piekarz is Senior Lecturer in Sport Management at the University of Worcester, UK. He has more than 25 years of experience in the sport management and adventure sport sectors and worked for many years as a sport facility manager and community sport development officer. He has published work on a variety of subject areas, ranging from risk management and sport and rights to conflict zone tourism and operational management.

The Basics

SPORT MANAGEMENT
THE BASICS

Rob Wilson and Mark Piekarz

LONDON AND NEW YORK

First published 2016
by Routledge
2 Park Square, Milton Park, Abingdon, Oxon, OX14 4RN

and by Routledge
711 Third Avenue, New York, NY 10017

Routledge is an imprint of the Taylor & Francis Group, an informa business

© 2016 Rob Wilson and Mark Piekarz

British Library Cataloguing-in-Publication Data
A catalogue record for this book is available from the British Library

Library of Congress Cataloging in Publication Data
Wilson, Robert.
Sport management : the basics / Robert Wilson & Mark Piekarz.
    pages cm. – (The Basics)
  Includes bibliographical references and index.
  1. Sports administration. I. Title.
  GV713.W55 2015
  796.06´9–dc23   2015011656

ISBN: 978-1-138-79116-9 (hbk)
ISBN: 978-1-138-79117-6 (pbk)
ISBN: 978-1-315-76299-9 (ebk)

Typeset in Bembo
by HWA Text and Data Management, London

CONTENTS

FIGURES

TABLES

BOXES

PREFACE

When we were approached to write a 'Basics' book on Sport Management our first thought was that given the number of generic sport management books on the market this book would simply get lost in a broader collection. What became very clear however was that while there are lots of books about sport management 'out there' they are all pitched at different levels of study, each of course having their relevant merits, but there was really nothing on the real 'basics'. What is sport management really about? How does the management of sport fit in today's ever complex society? And how can you make a career out of an industry so well-known for low pay, unsociable hours and, let's face it, an industry that is sometimes overshadowed by the impact of professional sports people who earn vast sums of money? Essentially these questions gave us a framework for this book. We wanted to produce a book which showcased what sport management was all about. How it was linked to many settings in our society, why you should study sport management in further and higher education and how you can make a great career in this fascinating industry.

We wanted to write a book that was accessible. A book that didn't assume that you knew anything about sport management, but one that can stimulate your interest to read on, to study and to work. We wanted to design a book for students and practitioners who want to understand the scale, diversity and importance of sport and how it can be managed.

It is not a book which explains in any detail how to manage sport better, or more effectively; that's left to that burgeoning collection we mentioned earlier. In any case, that would need a far more detailed book. Instead, we wanted to introduce you to the wide variety of sport-related activities, concepts and theories which can be considered part of the subject of sport management. It serves as an introduction to a variety of key concepts, theories and arguments which any student studying sport management, or indeed any practitioner involved with sport, should understand.

Whilst the term 'sport' has a superficial simplicity to it, often conjuring images of people playing and watching sport, this can belie how diverse and complex it can actually be. The mistake sometimes made in the past is that sport, because of its strong association with fun and enjoyment, can mean it is seen as less serious, even frivolous and less important than other areas of management, such as with banking or manufacturing.

The view that sport is not serious or deserving of a discrete and specialised area of management or study has now changed. This is evidenced by the scale and variety of sport being used as a form of popular and financially lucrative entertainment, whether this is in newspapers, watching games on TV or in pubs, attending an event, or even as the basis of computer games. It is evidenced by some of the remarkable qualities that are claimed about sport, whereby it is presented as a tool which can solve a wide variety of problems, ranging from improving people's health, bring about peace and reconciliation in war-torn communities, reduce crime, or create jobs. It is evidenced by the large number of academic courses relating to sport in general, or sport management in particular, which have grown around the world.

You may detect the use of the words 'claimed benefits' which suggest a degree of doubt about the ability of sport to 'do good'. You may also note the description of sport as a form of popular entertainment. This is done deliberately. One of the key challenges in writing this book was to work out how to break up the sport management industry for the purposes of study, so to that end we agreed on a set of themes.

These themes are not only intended to explain the breadth of sport management, but to challenge some of the simplistic arguments about the moral certitude that is often claimed about sport; that it is all good and virtuous; that to participate in it only brings benefits; that it can be life affirming and transformative; and that it is in some way ennobling and more than just entertainment to distract or pass time. Yes evidence can be found that it can do these good things, and many examples will be provided to illustrate this in this book; but then evidence can also be found that the impacts on people's lives can often be non-existent, minimal, or that sport can even be a source of various social and personal health problems.

If people are to be serious about the management of sport, then they cannot simply accept uncritically the arguments that sport is all good. These arguments must be analysed and evidenced. It is by doing this that a better understanding is gained of how sport can be used as a potential tool to do good, helping to develop more robust programmes and arguments of defence, rather than just the bland recycling of platitudes made by prominent sports people, politicians or heads of various governing sport bodies, which are then recycled and used as evidence by students and practitioners to justify sport programmes.

On a more personal level, if you reflect on a variety of sport experiences relating to the watching or playing of sport it can reveal some other interesting qualities about sport management. These reflections can also give an insight into what sport gives us, the inference being that this can begin to reveal how sport can potentially be a good thing. Just think of some of the most memorable sporting occasions which you have played in or watched. There is chance that you experienced a wide variety of emotions, ranging from elation, joy, to frustration and even anger, all of which can lead to an overall feeling of satisfaction or dissatisfaction. Remembered times are provocative emotional times. They form the benchmarks of our memory. Yet without the management and coordination of resources, the opportunity to experience these emotions would simply not take place.

At the heart of 'good' sport management should be this appreciation. An appreciation about why people want to play, watch, read, or buy sport-related products and services, which to understand properly needs to draw upon many scientific disciplines, such as economics, psychology and sociology. This in turn gives an understanding of a most basic question which a sport manager always needs to return to: just what are we providing the services and products for? Is it for profit? Is it to improve people's health? Is it to raise the prestige of a city or country? Whatever the answer, the academic study of sport management can help to find some answers.

It is from this understanding and insight into sport management that the business of designing and delivering appropriate management services can begin. To do this requires that: financial costs are considered; staff are coordinated, motivated and properly led; and job tasks are identified, tracked and monitored. How effectively these things are done can depend on the qualities of the person making the management decisions, which is why an important part of any sport management course (or book) is the process of reflecting upon decisions, in order to learn from mistakes, or know why actions are successful. To do this helps build a platform for future management successes.

Finally, it is vital for you to appreciate that because the word 'sport' is used that this creates some unifying aspect that means all sport management is the same. It is not. Someone brokering huge sponsorship contracts worth millions of pounds or dollars for a sporting mega-event, is very different from someone organising a grassroots sport programme which uses sport to rehabilitate former child soldiers in a country emerging from conflict. Sport is in there, somewhere, and you can identify some broad management ideas, such as the need to coordinate groups of people and resources, but the people really would be working in very different worlds. This attempt to constantly highlight key linking strands and the differences in various areas of sport management is a constant theme throughout this book and, much like the fact that sport is played across the globe, we have tried to provide as many global examples as we could think of.

In terms of how all these different themes discussed so far are brought through in different chapters, here is a short summary of the book structure.

- Chapter 1 gives an overview of the sport management industry, showing its diversity and to highlight what is unique about sport management, along with discussing how sport can be defined.
- Chapter 2 gives a broad historical overview of the development of the modern sport industry. It stresses the importance of the manager using history to remind them that change is a constant dynamic and past events and developments need critical scrutiny.
- Chapter 3 explores the management functional areas, skills and roles in general and more specifically for sport.
- Chapter 4 looks at the business functional areas, primarily focusing on the areas of marketing, finance and human resource management and how they can be used in a general sport-management role, or a more specialised one.
- Chapter 5 examines the levels of management and how they relate to each other, primarily explaining the levels of operational, project and strategic management.
- Chapter 6 explores the economics of the supply of sport to establish how and why certain sport services are provided.
- Chapter 7 focuses on the motivation and demand for sport goods and services. It is intimately entwined with marketing, stressing the vital importance of managers understanding consumers and customers' needs and wants.
- Chapter 8 essentially closes the book. Having explored a variety of concepts and ideas it is important that you understand where to go next. Consequently, this chapter brings together all of the ideas we have explored and is designed to encourage employment in the sector and encourage lifelong learning in this remarkable industry.

While the relevance of all is clear for a sport management student there is equal importance for students in other areas of study. The area of sport development, for example, and sport development officers (SDOs) has grown rapidly around the world, and much like sport management has many diverse functions. It should be appreciated that the work of a development officer can overlap between coaching and management. Indeed, when reading Chapter 2 on the history of sport, it should be evident that the early foundations of sport was a form of development work, whereby individuals and organisations often introduced sport into working-class communities, or sport into other countries: in all but name, it is development work. Indeed, many management functions in the voluntary and public sector have development-type work, sometimes adjusting their titles to fit into this newer area of sport, at other times not. Finally, it should also be appreciated that development work involves coordinating, organisation, communicating, leading and controlling, which in essence is about management.

These roles can often blur the distinctions between coaching, development and management roles, needing a discrete set of specific skills to either develop or expand a sport, or to develop individuals from their initial participation, to performing at an elite level.

In closing, we have written this book to give you a starting point. A point that you can lay the foundations and gain an understanding of the breadth of concepts which you will study on a sport management programme and that you will have to engage with over your years of study and early career. We hope that it can act as a starting point for many assignments, but can't promise that it will provide sufficient detail to complete a good-quality assignment, as you will need to read around your subject after all and one source of evidence is simply not enough. It does however give indications of what materials can be further examined in order to explore some of the theories and concepts in more depth.

Rob Wilson and Mark Piekarz

DEFINING SPORT, MANAGEMENT AND SPORT MANAGEMENT

INTRODUCTION

There often seems to be some sort of discussion around the juxtaposition of the terms 'sport' and 'business', particularly amongst those who struggle with the idea that 'business' brings with it feelings of 'enterprise', 'professionalism' and 'profit'. This link is particularly difficult when we factor in not-for-profit sport organisations and when we think about projects that are intended to develop sport for community engagement and recreational purposes. That said, the provision of sport and any function of sport, comes at a cost so the exploration of sport management, or even sport business management is important.

Sport management shares many generic characteristics with business operations. It requires the organisation of people, money and schedules. It can involve both the manufacturing of tangible goods, or the development of services. It can be a commercially lucrative sector, where brands can have global appeal, ranging from sport manufacturers, such as Nike and Adidas, to (in theory) non-commercial organisations, such as the International Olympic Committee (IOC) and the powerful, emblematic brand of the Olympic rings. It can operate in a complex global business environment, where change is a constant dynamic, or it can be used as a means to help support government welfare programmes and help achieve social policies. Sport, in short, can be big business which has continued to grow and needs to be managed like any other business.

So on one level sport is like any other business; it needs to pay its debts as they fall due and it needs to operate within its financial means and, like business in general, it can be studied and managed. Yet this argument works only so far. There are some important elements of sport which can mean it has some unique strands to it, which make it different and pose some important challenges for any manager working in this industry sector. More often than not though, sport *does not* and *has not* operated like 'normal' businesses. Just think for a moment how many times you read about professional sport clubs going into administration because of overspending. Furthermore, the fact that sport services are offered by commercial, profit-orientated organisations, or non-profit public and voluntary organisations, adds an additional layer of complexity which needs to be understood and explored.

Consequently, in this chapter we begin to explore the concepts of 'sport' and 'management'. This will help us to identify what is 'generic' and what is 'unique' to the area of 'sport management'. The chapter then moves on to illustrate just how diverse the sport industry can be, with the implication that sport management can have numerous possible variations, which will depend on things such as the sport that is focused on, whether the service is provided for profit, or to achieve a particular social objective, or indeed whether it can be further refined by being categorised as sport tourism, adventure sport, etc. Finally, we look at what is good about sport alongside some of the potential problems and issues that you may face.

WHAT IS SPORT?

In many ways, sport is easy to recognise. Sport is football, cricket, basketball, netball, athletics, rugby (both codes), swimming, rounders and hockey. Yet when we begin to explore the various definitions of sport, the picture can be more confusing, which then raises some interesting implications for the management of sport. Consider these two definitions of sport given by the Council of Europe and the Australian Commission for Sport (ASC):

> 'Sport' means all forms of physical activity which, through casual or organised participation, aim at expressing or improving physical fitness and mental well-being, forming social relationships or obtaining results in competition at all levels.
>
> (Council of Europe 2001)

> A human activity capable of achieving a result requiring physical exertion and/or physical skill which, by its nature and organisation, is competitive and is generally accepted as being a sport.
>
> (ASC 2014)

On the face of it, they seem clear enough. Sport is about physical activity or skill; it can be organised or competitive; and it can achieve some form of outcome. The Council of Europe definition gives more detail on what the ASC simply calls 'a result', by not only relating sport to physical activity, but also to its mental and social outcomes. These three outcomes, it should be noted, relate to the World Health Organization (WHO) definition of health as being 'a state of complete physical, mental and social well-being and not merely the absence of disease or infirmity' (WHO 2014). Both definitions also make the point that sport can often be competitive.

Roberts (2004, p. 81) offers four tests, which if an activity passes, can definitely be considered as sport. These tests are:

- sport are games separated from the rest of life by time, place and rules, where there is a desire to win;
- sport requires skill which can be improved upon;
- sports are energetic, which require physical exertion;
- sports are competitive, whether this is against other players or the clock.

Whilst actitivies such as football, netball, basketball or rugby would sit comfortably within such definitions, other activities such as climbing, skiing or surfing would not always fit so well, as there can be a strong individualistic, unstructured quality to them, with no formal written rules governing how people should participate. Yet many people would be comfortable to classify such activities as part of the sport industry, together with meeting the Council of Europe's much looser definition. Similarly, activities such as pool, snooker or darts have often been debated as to what extent they are, or should be considered as sport, but again when considered in relation to the Council of Europe's definition and the elements of 'skills' and the potential mental and social health benefits, they can be more comfortably defined as sport. Indeed, even looking at these games against Robert's four criteria, they may meet many of the criteria better than the activities such surfing, climbing or skiing, which for some may not feel quite right.

What these ambiguities and debates about what sport is, or should be, reveal that sport is a social construct. What this means is that different people, in different countries, at different times can define and understand sport in different ways, hence the potential for disagreement. Add into this mix a good dose of politics and ideology and one can get an even more confused picture. So what, you may ask? Such ambiguity and debate may seem unimportant and distracting from the practicalities of managing and working in the sport industry. This can be a mistake. In our mind there are three simple reasons why the difficulties of defining sport should be considered as important for managers to understand. These are:

1 *Developing analytical skills*: deciding what is and is not a sport demands analysis, reflection and an intellectual discussion, which helps give meaning and purpose to the activities. In one sense, it can be viewed as a form of mental gymnastics, where you need to explore and wrestle with the meaning of sport, which is helpful in developing a manager's analytical skill.

2 *Financial implications of funding and taxation:* on a more practical level, what is defined as sport can have implications for securing government or agency funding. In the UK, the sport-related government agency, Sport England, has the responsibility for allocating the money raised via the National Lottery for sport-related projects. The definition which they use is the Council of Europe definition, although they also acknowledge it can be a disputed term (Sport England, 2014a). The inference of this is that any activity which cannot meet some of the criteria of the definition will mean that they cannot be considered eligible for money from the different sport-funding streams.

3 *Sport activities are not a closed shop:* as the world changes and new technologies are developed, new activities have, and continue to emerge, which can challenge the existing status quo and cultural assumptions as to what sport is. Activities such as beach volleyball, snowboarding or BMX bike racing in the early stages of development were not seen as serious or somehow 'proper' sports as they challenged many existing cultural views and practices. Today, there is now far greater acceptance and recognition that these activities can be considered as sport, as evidenced by their inclusion as competitive events in the Olympic Games.

This last point about not being a closed shop, where new sport activities can be developed, is particularly important in relation to sport management. What it reveals is the dynamic nature of sport, where changes in society, the economy and new technological innovations have constantly helped develop and grow new sports (or erode the participation in older ones). This raises some interesting future challenges for sport managers. An example of how an activity such as competitive computer gaming challenges our understanding of sport is considered in Box 1.1.

There is one other important point to make when considering sport definitions in relation to sport management. The definitions of sport focus on the 'doing', the 'playing', and the 'participation'; but sport management is much more than this, as it can involve manufacturing goods, or staging sport

BOX 1.1   CAN COMPUTER GAMES EVER BE CONSIDERED A SPORT OR PART OF THE SPORT INDUSTRY?

Sport has certainly been used for the basis of many popular computer games, ranging from soccer, ice hockey, golf and cricket, not to mention the emergence of application-based games that can be driven via a smartphone and incorporate a gambling platform, which can allow in-play betting whilst watching live sport events. The market for these types of games is significant and difficult to fully quantify. Whilst arguments can be made that they can form part of the sport industry, a much more difficult question to ask is whether they can ever actually be considered as sports? The development by Nintendo of the Wii console and various games, such as Wii Sports, which involved greater physical activity and participation, gives one angle to explore the issue of whether they can ever be considered as sport. These are, however, still set within the home and although other gaming manufacturers have continued to develop the physical element, they are perhaps still at best considered as active recreation activities.

Perhaps more intriguing and challenging to what sport can be relates to the growth in the number of competitive gaming events around the world. Major League Gaming competitions have become big business, allowing for people to make a professional living by competing. It can involve a variety of computer games which people can train for and compete in. Whilst there can be a simplistic stereotype of the lonely computer gamer, who has irregular sleep patterns, a poor diet and does not 'get out' enough, this can be challenged, whereby the large gaming events demonstrate that they can also create many social opportunities, be highly stimulating and can increasingly involve physical activity. As the technology and the gaming rules develop some intriguing questions are raised about what are sometimes described as virtual sports. Indeed, there are now a number of professional teams around the world, who have clear training schedules in terms of playing games and maintaining their own physical fitness (parallels can be made with racing drivers, where the superficial appearance is that it is a sedentary activity, but one which in fact requires an incredible level of physical fitness). Looking at the growing numbers of professional gamers and how they train and play, they can meet the various definitions of sport quite easily, including Roberts' (2004) four tests, but for many they would not be comfortable as accepting them as sports.

Whilst at present the cultural construction of sport is such that many would not define competitive gaming as sport, a simple look back at history and how new activities on their first introduction were not initially accepted or considered as sport, illustrate how things can change. For example, when snowboarding began to emerge in the 1970s, many skiers attempted to ban it (indeed, some resorts did) often based on some spurious safety argument, when in fact it was a much simpler case of the 'new' challenging the 'old'. Yet by 1998 snowboarding had become an Olympic event, which gave the activity an official seal of approval for its status as a sport. The IOC has increasingly shown a willingness to engage with activities which can have a stronger appeal to young people, which leads to an intriguing question as to whether virtual gaming in the future can sit more comfortably with a definition of sport.

The point to emphasise about all these examples is that they are examples of change. A change which challenges many old, preconceived attitudes and ways of doing things. And for any sport manager, change will be a constant dynamic in their working environment which good managers will adapt to, rather than just resist.

events for passive consumption, at least in a physical and skill sense. The danger therefore is that if one is too prescriptive and narrow as to what is sport, it can give a misleading and limited understanding of what sport management actually is.

WHAT IS MANAGEMENT?

A more detailed examination of what management is will be explored in later chapters. For now, what needs to be considered is something that helps achieve a basic understanding of its key principles. Over the past hundred years or so, a rich and diverse range of literature has developed about management and, perhaps more importantly, what factors make for good management. Naturally, it is beyond the scope of this book to look in detail at this historical development of management theory and all the key writers, but aspects are returned to in Chapter 3. For now, just a few of the key concepts which many books on management utilise will suffice. One classic, often cited definition as to what management is given by Mary Parker Follet (1918), who simply defined management as: 'management is the art of getting things done through people'. The brevity of this statement gives clarity to one of the essential qualities of management. But more is needed to give a better understanding of the scope of what management involves. Fayol is another key early writer on management, with his work (for example, 1916) providing a key foundation for later writers on management. His identification of five key areas of management are ones commonly cited in many management texts, referring to:

- *planning:* establishing direction and aims, goals or objectives for the organisation and the activity;
- *organising:* organising the resources, such as people, to try and achieve the objectives identified in the plan;
- *commanding staff:* direct staff to try and achieve the objectives (adjusted to 'communication' in this book in later references);
- *coordinating:* teams of people and resources are coordinated in order to effectively achieve the objectives, as efficiently as possible;
- *controlling:* monitoring progress and performance, making changes in teams and resources as needed in order to achieve the objective.

Whilst terms such as 'commanding' may not sit so well with more contemporary management cultures, where the term suggests a rigid hierarchical flow of information and direction, from the top to the bottom, the areas still give a useful and simple summary of some of the key features of management. Features which are just as applicable to anyone involved in the sport sector, as in any other business sector. In Chapter 3, these areas of management are explored in more detail, where a variety of questions are considered.

A simple sport analogy can be given to illustrate how these concepts might be used by a football or soccer team manager. The *plan* relates to winning games, which leads to winning titles and trophies. To achieve this plan a strategy may be worked out at the beginning of the season, such as identifying players to buy, developing new training facilities, programmes etc. The manager will then *organise* the teams on the field and the supporting staff to help the players perform better. On the field, the manager will issue *commands* of what he wants players to do in order to try and win the game. He will also need to ensure the team is *coordinated* and balanced. As the game is played, the performance is monitored, with the manager making any changes as they see fit, so they are continuing to try and *control* the effort put in by the team.

THE DIVERSITY OF SPORT MANAGEMENT

The discussion so far should show that sport management is not quite as simple and obvious as may have been first thought. To further help reveal the complexity and diversity of what sport management can potentially involve, a variety of additional factors can be considered, summarised in Figure 1.1.

Here is a short description of what each category in Figure 1.1 refers to:

• *Generalist or the specialist:* this relates to whether a manager has a specialist function in the sport business, such as working in sales, marketing or financial management, or is a generalist, where they may do a 'bit of everything' relating to operations, marketing and financial management. Whilst for a large, multinational organisations, there will be opportunities for more specialist functions within an organisational structure, for a manager of a small sport enterprise or facility, they will have to have an understanding of many management and business functional areas.

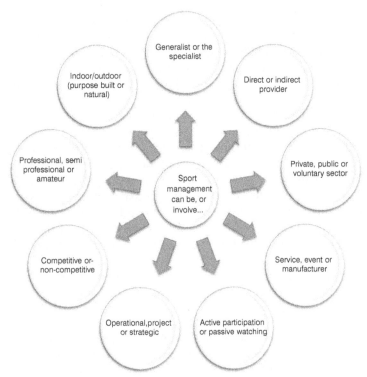

Figure 1.1   An overview of different areas/types of sport management

- *Direct or indirect provider:* sport activities provide many direct management responsibilities, such as managers designing sport programmes taking place in a sport facility or gym. In turn, and in order for these activities to take place, there can be a need to purchase various goods and services, such as clothing, racquets, balls or transport. The people who supply these goods and services can be considered as part of the indirect or secondary sport industry. Gambling offers another interesting example of a sector which has an indirect role in terms of actual sport activities and events.
- *Private, public or voluntary sector:* sport services can be provided by three key supply sectors: the private sector which operates for commercial gain or profit; the public sector

which provides services to achieve social objectives, such as improving people's health (see the next section for more details); and the voluntary or, as it is sometimes called, the third sector, which may be involved with achieving social objectives, or to just allow people to play (discussed in more detail in Chapter 6).

- *Service, event or manufacturer*: the sport industry can involve managers operating in the manufacturing sector, such as producing sport clothing and equipment. It can involve the design and provision of services, such as keep-fit sessions in a gym, or grassroots sport coaching activities for children. It can involve the management and staging of sport events, which can vary in scale, ranging from small community sport days, to the huge mega-events, such as the Olympics. Each area, again providing for their own set of challenges.

- *Active participation or passive watching:* managers can be involved with providing services and events which can have a more passive element (in a physical sense, not necessarily an emotional one), where it is about the watching of sport, compared with the physical participation in the sport. We'll come back to this in Chapter 7.

- *Operational, project or strategic:* simply put, there are three broad levels that managers can operate within. At an operational level, this involves management activities which help deliver direct services, or ensure that goods are made on time. At the strategic level, the scale of the resources which need to be coordinated and the timescales focused on can be much larger. Project management tends to fall between the operational and strategic level, but has the key distinguishing feature that there is a clear start and end point to the work. These themes are returned to in Chapter 5.

- *Competitive or non-competitive:* sport managers can be involved with providing sport services which can involve competitive elements to them, which can range from organising leagues, racing events, to more free-form activities, such as climbing, or cycling. There are also quasi-competitive events, such as the growth of the park run phenomenon, where local communities stage regular five-kilometre running events which are principally concerned with the promotion of organised physical activity, yet routinely pitch runners against themselves to achieve better individual times week-on-week.

- *Professional, semi-professional or amateur:* whilst the image of a professional athlete may resonate most in people's minds, they can distract from the true scale of the industry and the breadth of entrepreneurial opportunities which exist for the semi-professional, amateur or complete novice sport person. Examples of services here can range from offering tailor-made training packages to increase elite athlete performance in sport resorts, or a personal trainer helping someone getting fit for a race which they are undertaking to raise money or, simply for their own personal satisfaction of overcoming a challenge.

- *Indoor/outdoor (purpose-built or natural):* there is a huge variety in the number and size of facilities which need to be managed. Ultimately this poses management challenges and can need specialist knowledge. For example, sport stadiums and indoor sport arenas need careful consideration of various regulations relating to safety (e.g. health and safety regulations, fire regulations etc.); outdoor pitches for soccer, hockey and rugby can be natural or artificial, and are exposed to natural hazards such as the weather, which need to be risk assessed, and specialist maintenance programmes and staff. Sometimes, the sport activity can take place in a completely natural setting, such as cross-country running events, trekking, climbing, or surfing.

When examining these different categories, it should be appreciated that management roles can be mixed up in many different ways, depending on the size and scale of the organisation, or the skills and attributes of the manager. They should also illustrate the sheer breadth and potential diversity which exists in sport management (a number of which are explored in more detail in Chapter 8). Here are two examples to illustrate how these different categories can be mixed up, based on real jobs which were advertised, and presented in Table 1.1.

Table 1.1   Examples of two jobs to illustrate the variety of sport management

Example of a generalist manager	Example of a specialist manager
A job advertised for a duty manager for a small, UK sport facility involves working for a charitable trust (third sector) called Impulse Leisure, who manage a sport facility owned by the local government (public sector). This role is primarily operational, as it involves the day-to-day safe running of the facilities. The job would serve customers who fit into the novice to amateur level of performance, for primarily non-competitive activities, as the facility offers services relating to people working out in a gym or swimming. Periodically, they may become involved with project management, such as putting together a funding strategy to help renovate part of the sport facility. The manager would also be an example of the generalist, rather than the specialist, and is service based.	A ticket sales coordinator (general public) was advertised by UEFA, who in theory could be classed as a third sector operator. However, their strong commercial drive can mean they often blur into the private sector, given their profit-generating activities. The job involves implementing and managing the ticket sales process for the UEFA Euro 2016 soccer event to be held in France. The role spans all three management levels, in that it has many strategic elements to it in relation to the scale of resources which need to be coordinated, and the timescales planned for. It is also project based in that it has a clear start and end time. As the time nears for the release of tickets sales, it will become more operationally based in order to ensure the smooth selling of tickets. It is an example of a different type of specialist management role focusing on tickets for a football event, but needs an understanding of financial management, human resources and marketing.

What these different elements also illustrate is that sport is very much a composite industry: that is to say, to play sports, or to stage sport events, involves drawing together a wide variety of business products and services. The implication in terms of sport management is that there are numerous opportunities to be involved with sport directly, or in many supporting indirect secondary markets.

SPORT LEISURE, RECREATION, EVENTS, TOURISM AND ADVENTURE – EVEN MORE SECTORS

It can be important for many sport managers to think beyond sport itself. This may seem strange (particularly as this is a sport management book), but for some areas of sport management, it can be vital to appreciate how, for example, sport venues can be used for other non-sporting activities and purposes which can help generate additional revenue, or help achieve a variety of social objectives. A simple example relates to how sport halls or stadiums can be used for music concerts. Alternatively, with some sport development projects, where there are limited resources and facilities, it can relate to how non-sport spaces can be used for sport or active recreational activities. More examples are given in Box 1.2.

To further help this process of sport managers not just thinking about sport, it is useful to consider sport's relationship with a number of related industry sectors, primarily the leisure, recreation, events, tourism and adventure sectors, presented in Figure 1.2. To do this can help prevent the sport manager becoming myopic (i.e. closed- or narrow-minded) and failing to see opportunities and threats which may be emerging from other areas.

What Figure 1.2 illustrates is how each of the concepts have their own distinct attributes, but also many characteristics which are shared. Here is a summary of what each concept refers to and the relationship to sport management:

- *Leisure:* leisure can be understood in a variety of ways. Torkildsen (2005) provides a very useful discussion about what is leisure, noting how it can be defined in relation to: time free from obligated activities, such as work; as an experience and how it makes a person feel, or a state of mind and being; or it can relate to time spent on self-development and improvement, which is much closer to the original, ancient classical Greek ideal (discussed in Chapter 2). Sport has an intimate association with leisure, as it is one of the ways to spend enjoyable time, which has the potential to improve a person in some way. Obviously, not all leisure is sport, as leisure is a much broader concept, which can involve activities ranging from visiting the cinema, being engaged with hobbies, or even do-it-yourself (DIY) home projects. Equally, it can be questioned whether playing sport, such as with professional sport people, should be classified as a leisure activity, as it can deemed as their work.

BOX 1.2   THE IMPORTANCE OF SPORT MANAGERS NOT JUST THINKING ABOUT SPORT

The Olympic Games is symbiotic with sporting excellence. Yet it should be appreciated how staging the games is not just about the actual sporting spectacle that runs over a number of weeks. Since the rebirth of the Olympic Games in 1894, part of the philosophical foundation of the movement has always been about both physical and intellectual development and celebration. As a result, the sporting event has often been accompanied by a cultural event. How big these cultural festivals have been is varied, but it is noticeable that, as the cost of staging the games has increased, the level of justification needs to be strengthened by showing how many different groups in society can benefit. For example, at the London Games millions was spent on numerous art projects around the UK, ranging from commissioned art works to the world Shakespeare festival which ran throughout 2012. Even the opening ceremony, directed by the film director Danny Boyle, can claim to have been a more of a cultural celebration rather than just a sporting one.

This consideration beyond sport has also become very much part of the thinking (in theory) about the legacies of large sport events. The 2014 Football World Cup in Brazil, for example, received some high profile criticism over the creation of stadiums, built at a substantial cost, yet would only host four games; however the Arena das Dunas stadium in the city of Natal, was praised by FIFA as an example of good, flexible design, where its capacity could be varied between 30,000 to 40,000, due to its open end and temporary seating. This has meant the stadium can be used for other non-sporting events, such as music concerts.

By contrast, someone involved in sport development or outreach work, may have a remit to try and improve the health of a local community. Sport could be used, but awareness should be had by the manager or sport development officer (SDO) that some people may have many negative connotations about sport and find it off-putting, so a far better emphasis could be on physical and mental active recreation, such as organising walking groups or dance classes. The final outcome is what is important, not necessarily that people play sport, which some managers working in community sport may have to consider.

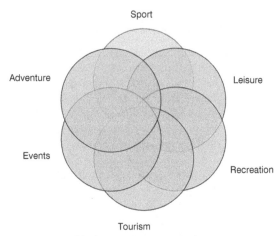

Sport

Adventure

Leisure

Events

Recreation

Tourism

Figure 1.2   An overview of the key sectors sport can relate to

- *Recreation:* recreation is a term which has fallen out of favour in recent times and has arguably been replaced by sport and physical activity. It has an intimate relationship with leisure, often used interchangeably (Taylor 2012, p. 13), with the central idea of recreation referring to how it can help a person 're-create' themselves being of critical importance. The notion that doing certain activities can in some way restore, renew or revive a person should be an attractive quality for many sport managers to think about in terms of designing sport services, particularly when at times it may be better to focus on a concept of active recreation rather than sport as noted in Box 1.2.
- *Events:* sport events are big business and because they can receive so much media exposure, they represent an area that many will initially think of when the term sport management is referred to. It is important though to consider how events can be bigger than just sport, or, alternatively, how sport events and venues must think beyond sport, as Box 1.2 illustrates. This is particularly true for those managing facilities where the sport event can give a stadium its core service, but flexibility and creativity is needed to consider how it can be used for other purposes, ranging from music concerts, religious gatherings and exhibition events.

- *Tourism:* tourism is a major global industry, which can easily be considered as the largest service industry sector in the world. Tourism encompasses the sectors of transport, accommodation, food, beverages and attractions. In terms of the basis of attractions, these can range from beaches, historical buildings and monuments and, increasingly, sport activities and events. Over recent years sport tourism has become a more discrete subject area and important growth market, whereby people will travel and stay away from home for more than 24 hours to either attend sport events, or to participate in sport activities, such as marathons, triathlons, bike events etc. The emergence of low-cost airlines has also increased the market for short city breaks, which in turn has grown the market for people visiting famous sport stadiums, such as the Nou Camp in Barcelona, or the Bernabeu in Madrid.

- *Adventure:* adventure has been another flourishing sector of tourism, but it has its own discrete attributes, such as its long history of being used as means for education and personal development. This can relate to the many outdoor facilities that operate for schools and corporate team-building, or even with the global 'Scout' movement. What is of interest in relation to sport, is how part of the adventure sector has been a key driver of many new activities, where the boundaries between sport and adventure can be blurred. Events such as the X Games have steadily grown in terms of participation, media coverage and sponsorship, taking place now for both winter and summer events. The range of activities or sports which take place are diverse, ranging from mountain biking, moto racing, skateboarding, climbing and BMX racing for the summer games, and snow-boarding, snow mountain bike racing and ice climbing for the winter events. Adventure activities can also take place in both natural, unaltered settings, or urban, purpose-built facilities, such as indoor climbing centres, skate and biking venues, or even the 'Playmania' indoor ski centre in Dubai.

WHAT IS DIFFERENT ABOUT SPORT MANAGEMENT?

We argued earlier, perhaps paradoxically, that sport is like any other business, and so can use generic management theories and business; yet it is also noted that at times, sport has some unique features, which means it is not quite like any other business. Two key themes will be identified and discussed here in relation to what makes sport management more distinct, or gives a particular set of challenges different from other business areas. The first relates to the rhetoric (i.e. the language and arguments used) that sport is something good, which has the power to transform societies and individuals for the better. It is a claim which cannot go uncontested, hence the later consideration given to how sport can be bad. The second key theme relates to how sport businesses do not always behave or obey some of the normal rules of the free market because of the distorting effects of emotional attachment.

THE BENEFITS OF SPORT

It is easy to find statements about how good and virtuous playing and watching sport can be. This statement from the UN cites a quite breathtaking array of benefits, saying:

> Sport is far more than a luxury or a form of entertainment. Access to and participation in sport is a human right and essential for individuals of all ages to lead healthy and fulfilling lives. Sport – from play and physical activity to organised competitive sport – has an important role in all societies. Sport is critical to a child's development. It teaches core values, such as cooperation and respect. It improves health and reduces the likelihood of disease. It is a significant economic force providing employment and contributing to local development. And, it brings individuals and communities together, bridging cultural or ethnic divides. Sport offers a cost-effective tool to meet many development and peace challenges, and helps achieve the MDGs.
>
> (UN 2005, p.1)

These are some remarkable claims. As a business and social activity, you would be hard-pressed to find another similar example which has so many virtuous attributes. Attributes which have become a key rhetoric often pounced on by event organisers, governing bodies, politicians and students, who are looking for ways to build an argument, in order to justify that money spent by governments on sport projects represents good value, or will generate a return on investment. An overview of some of the key arguments about the claimed benefits of sport is presented in Table 1.2.

The evidence for these gains can be patchy to say the least, but some examples can be used to illustrate the potential benefits. Research commissioned to show the benefits

Table 1.2   A summary of the claimed benefits of sport and sport events

Category	Examples of the claimed benefits
Economic benefits	Improved economic activity; employment opportunities; facilities and stadiums acting as engines to drive regeneration of poor or deprived areas; improvements in health and well-being which in turn can increase productivity; helping poor countries achieve the millennium development goals (MDGs).
Social benefits	Reduction in crime, delinquency and other social problems; instils pride; builds community confidence; helps integration of groups; education (e.g. the attempts to use sport to educate about diseases, such as the Kick It Out campaign in football, or the Slam Dunking Aids programme in basketball); education about issues of racism, sexism and homophobia.
Political	Peace and reconciliation; opportunity for political leverage to raise issues of human rights; point of leverage to initiate political change; enhance human rights; expressions of liberty; nation-building (e.g Mandela's use of sport as part of the reconciliation process after years of apartheid); rebranding and reimaging cities, regions and countries; statements of political power.
Environment	Regeneration of poor sites; green agenda promoted; benchmarking of good practice.
Individual health and personal development	Improve physical, mental and social health and wellbeing; development of leadership skills; moral leadership; rehabilitation; courage; good citizenship; confidence building; catharsis (venting of frustrations and anger).
Inspiration and role models	Watching high levels of performance inspire people to play; athletes can act as role models to aspire to for moral development and leadership.

of physical activity (note not simply sport) to mental and physical health can be found in a variety of journal articles. For example, Biddle and Mutrie (2008) give a useful overview of the various pieces of research which point to the benefits of physical activity, which sport can potentially make an important contribution to. Other, different examples of the possible benefits can be found elsewhere. For example, in 1995 Nelson Mandela sought to use the Rugby World Cup as an opportunity to unite the nation of South Africa and begin to defuse racial tension that had fragmented the country. Mandela went to great lengths to ensure that the South African team, who won the tournament, was not viewed as a win for white South Africans but a win for the nation and all its people, white or black. Other examples can relate to how charities have targeted events, particularly to raise the issue of child labour. During the 1998 Football World Cup in France, groups such as Christian Aid used the event to show how many of the footballs and garments were made by exploiting child labour and by 2006 FIFA showed that it had at least in some way engaged with the issue, with its pledge to fight such exploitation of child labour (FIFA 2006).

CONTESTING THE BENEFITS

So one of the key distinguishing features about sport can be its endowment of some powerful, transformative, almost mythical powers to do good. These attributes are one of the elements which can make sport management very different from other areas of business, which must be understood and managed.

These stated benefits, summarised in Table 1.2, *must not* be accepted without question. If you are serious about sport management then you should not simply use a statement about the power of sport to do good, uttered by powerful world leaders, or any other prominent individual as evidence that sport actually achieves these things. To blindly accept that sport is all good and all powerful is to run the danger that you become a manager who patronises target groups, is parsimonious in management (i.e. someone who is closed-minded and ungenerous), and is divorced from the realities of how useful and effective sport projects really are to achieve a variety of social objectives.

The problem we find with this is that the examples of good can be, and often are, anecdotal, used selectively and suffer the problem, which Coalter (2013, p. 13 citing Wagner 1964), calls the 'displacement of scope'. The displacement of scope argument refers to people generalising the potential beneficial micro-effects of sport activities, to other larger sport projects; that is to say, for example, because evidence can be found that an individual has experienced health benefits playing sport, this does not mean any health benefits will automatically accrue by staging a sport event. The two are different things, so evidence cannot be transferred between them. Indeed, the sport event whilst it may help with social health needs, it can be bad for physiological health as it may encourage the passive viewing and consumption of take-out, fatty food, alcohol and sugary drinks. To further illustrate how for each cited positive benefit, it is possible to counter it with a potential problem, a variety of examples are given in Table 1.3, which mirrors the broader categories presented earlier in Table 1.2.

Many of the examples of the problems presented in Table 1.3 are designed to be provocative and challenging. Hopefully, many of you will disagree with them and if this is the case then you are engaging with the process of analysis, which will drive you to find the evidence to refute the arguments.

THE DISTORTING EFFECT OF EMOTIONS ON SPORT MANAGEMENT

A second key feature which distinguishes sport management is how the strong emotional connection and attachments which key stakeholders can have with sport teams and activities can have a profound impact on behaviour and decision-making. In Europe, for example, many football clubs have deep roots in their communities, with teams emerging from such diverse areas as factories, breweries or churches. Although many of the original founding organisations and businesses have gone, the

Table 1.3   Examples of the problems of sport

Category	Examples of possible problems
Economic benefits	Many stadiums built for major events have failed to have a sustainable legacy, such as the Athens Olympic Stadium. Spending on sport can also lead to increased taxation, or the economic benefits are reduced because of the influence of global multinational enterprises, as more money 'leaks' out of the local economy.
Social benefits	Sport can divide and segregate communities; for mega-events such as the Olympic Games, or soccer World Cup, it has sometimes meant residents have been forcibly moved out of their homes in order to build new stadiums and infrastructure; it can lead to inflation of land prices, increasing inequalities.
Political	Whilst an event such as Olympic Games helped act as a trigger to support reform in South Korea, moving from an authoritarian regime to a democracy, in China it seemed to reinforce the power base of the authoritarian government; governments placing restrictions of freedoms, such as where they can protest; states using force to allow events to take place, which can sometimes lead to abuses of human rights.
Environment	Environments can be damaged as much as they may be protected; huge movements of people travelling to events can increase global carbon emissions that would otherwise not have occurred.
Individual health and personal development	Playing sport can cause injuries, which is a cost to health services; people transferring skills learnt in sport, such as team work, leadership etc, can have very mixed results when transferring these skills to more mainstream work environments (or student group assignments); stadium disasters have shown how commercial pressures to save money and cut costs are done at the expense of people's safety; sport events can encourage poor lifestyles.
Inspiration and role models	Sport can show how people cheat to win at all costs; elite athletes are not normal or typical of the rest of society, so are not representative role models; people can watch sport, but they may be no more likely to go out and play sport, than watching a film, will want to make them go out and act.

teams and the clubs remain, with their names and emblems often showing signs of their heritage. The result is that deep emotional connections are formed, where the football club forms an intimate part of the identity of the individual and community; a connection which means that even though many football clubs may no longer be viable commercial businesses, operating with huge debts and making consistent

BOX 1.3   FOOTBALL CLUBS WHICH IGNORE THE RULES OF THE MARKET

The intimate association sport clubs have with their fans can mean that even when they are mismanaged, or carry huge debts, they can continue to exist, when for any other businesses they would have long gone out of business. We can point to many examples across the football pyramid in various countries to illustrate this. One high-profile case related to the demise of Portsmouth Football Club, officially the first club to play in the English Premier League to enter administration. Other parts of the United Kingdom operate in a similar way, with Glasgow Rangers football club, one of the biggest clubs in Scotland, which consistently won the Scottish League and many cups, becoming bankrupt in 2012 when a creditors' report revealed quite astonishing levels of debt (in excess of £130 million). This forced the club into administration and ultimately liquidation. For any other business, that would have been the end. For Glasgow Rangers and their fans it meant the club being reformed as a new company and re-applying for membership to the Scottish football league, entering into the Fourth Division for the 2012–2013 season.

There are many examples of other clubs who have performed poorly as a business yet continue to be saved, normally by wealthy benefactors that can stomach large losses due to deep pockets. The model is unsustainable and governing bodies are taking action through the introduction of Financial Fair Play regulations designed to ensure clubs break even. These regulations are essentially in place to protect fans, whose club means so much to them, being undermined by poor business decisions.

In Germany, the case of FC Union Berlin which was part of East Germany under communist control shows the powerful connection fans can have. After the threats of closure of the outdated stadium which would jeopardise any promotional prospects, the decision was made to modernise that stadium. As resources were limited, around 2,000 fans volunteered to help, quite literally, rebuild the stadium. After 11 months and thousands of hours of work done on a voluntary basis, the stadium was ready for the team which had won promotion to the second division of the Bundesliga.

financial losses, they somehow manage to ignore the normal rules of the free market and continue to operate. Examples of this unusual relationship are further explored in Box 1.3.

CONCLUSION

It can be tempting to see that because the word 'sport' appears with the word 'management' that this refers to a coherent, single, simple sector. Hopefully, you may have found during this introductory chapter that sport management is much more diverse and larger than you initially suspected. If so, this chapter has done what it set out to. In terms of management, just what can be managed has numerous variations, ranging from manufacturing of goods, designing services, managing facilities, marketing etc. Furthermore, sport is a composite industry, which supports numerous other industrial sectors, from transport, accommodation, catering, clothing and, in particular, the media. To be involved in the sport industry, can mean that no ball is kicked, no shorts are worn, no running has taken place, but those who do these things, are as reliant on others to help print the tickets, to make the clothes, to take them from A to B.

This chapter has shown how sport can be like any other business, which needs to draw on the key concepts, theories and disciplines of business management. What makes sport different and can pose some important management challenges relate to the belief it can be a force for good, and that the emotional connection with sport can skew behaviour. Caution is emphasised that the arguments for good are not simply recycled, with no consideration of the evidence for them, or how benefits which may be found in one sport project can actually be transferred to another.

2

A HISTORY OF
SPORT MANAGEMENT

INTRODUCTION

We've designed this chapter to give you a brief historical overview of how the sport industry has developed in the UK and abroad. Some sport managers may not see the value of examining history, as it may seem to offer little help in the actual and immediate management of sport businesses. This chapter will explain why this attitude is wrong! The value of examining sport history is that it gives a vital reminder that 'change' generated by the external business environment, whether that is political, social, technological or economic, is a constant dynamic which managers must deal with, to help them seize opportunities, counter threats, capitalise on strengths or manage weaknesses. It will also help managers to reflect on current and future management practices so that they can help their business or organisation grow.

We begin this chapter by explaining the value to sport managers of having an understanding of the history of how the sport industry has evolved and grown. Following this we move onto a very broad sweep of some key historical developments in relation to both sport activities and the philosophy of sport. The periods of industrialisation is given particular attention (in the context of the UK) as this is the crucial period and country for understanding the early origins of many sports which dominate the world today.

THE VALUE OF HISTORY

History, it must be stressed, is not simply listing past historical events. At its most basic level, history is the study or investigation of the human past. Good history involves not just an attempt to identify and examine historical facts, but should also explore the more complex relationships of past events and peoples' actions, which may involve looking at 'why' people acted the way they did and 'what' the consequences were. The study of history, as Carr (1961, p. 87) argues, is the study of causes and asking the question 'why?', whereby the answer should not be given by way of a single causation fact, but by multiple causation factors, properly organised and interpreted. History, in short, involves a critical analysis of the past.

An important part of studying history is recognising that past historical writing can always be challenged and views change (Carr 1961, p. 89). The result is that history can change. This may seem nonsensical to some and you would be right to ask 'how can the past change'? The reality is that people write history, which can be influenced by what facts and events they select as evidence, which can be distorted and shaped by their own biases, be challenged by new evidence, or simply be examined and written in different ways as new questions are asked. For the sport manager, this acts as a reminder that what may be initially be accepted as certainties and truth, can often have the potential to change.

Some sport managers and many students studying sport may still struggle to understand the full relevance of history to management. For them, the focus for management should be on the here and now, or what needs to be done in the future. To look at the past may seem pointless and a distraction from immediate and long-term decision-making. In fact the complete opposite can be argued. The earlier summary of what relates to good history should be utilised as one of the principles of what makes for good management: the critical analysis of the past, in order to try and learn from past mistakes and incidents and make better future management decisions. Adopting an historical approach is invaluable for showing how and why sport is a social construct, which has always changed, and will continue to change in the future. Examples of this were given in Chapter 1, when the different definitions of sport were discussed and how political, economic, social and technological changes have influenced what is understood by the word 'sport'.Gemmell (2011, p. 711), in his discussion on the history of cricket, comments that it is a 'lazy historian' who does not consider the wider social, political and economic forces which have shaped sport; so too for sport management, whereby it is the 'lazy sport manager' who does not consider how past environmental factors have shaped their organisation, sport and industry. You must look back at what has gone before to make things better in the future.

Here are some additional factors to consider which help show the value of history for the sport manager:

- *It shows that change is constant:* the industrialisation process of the eighteenth and nineteenth centuries is a critical period in shaping many contemporary sport industries and practices. The later section in this chapter on industrialisation give a number of powerful examples of how changing political, economic, social and technological forces (i.e. the PEST layers of the external business environment discussed in Chapter 5) radically transformed sport, with some sport organisations embracing the opportunities and surviving and flourishing, whilst those that did not, withered and disappeared. It is a process of change which has not slowed, instead becoming ever more rapid and complex. Understanding these changes should remind a manager that the business conditions are rarely static (even though it can feel that way at times) and that they are always in a process of change.
- *It can help guard against the risk of organisations suffering from facility inertia and orientation:* for businesses operating in

the private sector, one of the key indicators of whether they should provide a service or good is whether it is profitable. This means, in theory, there is an inherent dynamic and pressure for change, whereby if past services are not profitable, they will no longer be offered, with new, more attractive services created. For services offered by the public and voluntary sector (discussed in Chapter 6), this mechanism for change has not always been as relevant (although this is changing), where the rationale for providing services is to achieve various non-profit social objectives, which can lead to what Coalter (1990, p. 3) describes as 'facility inertia' or Torkildsen's (2005, p. 134) argument of 'facility orientation'. The result is unthinking, uncritical organisational inertia, whereby both financial and cultural practices are based on past practices and philosophical outlooks, often going back to the nineteenth century.

- *It reveals that organisational cultures and individual values are variable and change over time:* examining how sports have changed shows how transitory and historically variable (Coalter 1990, p. 3) many of our views can be. Some of the arguments used in the past to prevent change can now appear racist, sexist, at best misguided, often just plain stupid, a number of which are looked at later. The historian Eric Hobsbawn's work on the invention of traditions, gives numerous examples of how various sport rituals which can appear as ancient, are often more recent creations (Hobsbawn and Ranger 2012). For example, the emblematic torch-carrying procession of the Olympic Games was an invention of the 1936 Munich Games, not really part of some more ancient tradition.
- *It shows that change must be managed, not simply fought and resisted:* looking back at the development of many sports, the number of instances that people resisted and fought changes can be striking, many of which they would ultimately be powerless to stop. Looking at these examples can give a point for reflection for the contemporary manager and whether their present actions and views will be seen as dynamic risk-taking, which drives change, or

simply conservative inertia, resisting change. Examples of this were given in Chapter 1, with more given later in this section.

- *It shows the motivation for games and sport has always been there, but the expressions and forms change over time:* looking at the past shows how the human desire to play games can meet many intrinsic or basic human needs (we discuss this in more detail in Chapter 7). Running, throwing and jumping could be rooted in hunting and fighting (Collins 2013, p. 1), or religious ceremonies, or games which can be used to learn, develop or master environments. All illustrate an innate desire to play, but are shaped by the society we are in and the technologies available.

- *It can be used for comparative country analysis to help evaluate future markets:* we can use the past to give an insight into present-day sport-consumption patterns. The level of economic development will always be a key performance measure, particularly in relation to sustaining the watching, participation and consumption of sport goods and services. However, we should never underestimate the importance of how cultures shape a desire for play and entertainment. History helps answer the question of why football is the largest sport in many South American countries, but not in the USA, Australia or India. It can help reveal some of the institutional problems of racism or sexism in sport. This knowledge can then be used to try and develop marketing strategies to strengthen a sport's market position, working out how to enter new markets, generate profit or achieve broader social objectives (See Chapter 7 for examples).

- *It encourages deeper analysis of causation factors:* when dealing with present-day problems, it can be worthwhile exploring more deeply the roots of the problem. An insight into this is given in the case study in Box 2.1. This helps demonstrate the importance of examining past incidents as part of the management process of risk management.

BOX 2.1 WHY STUDY THE PAST? THE HILLSBOROUGH CASE STUDY

History is not the mere reporting of facts but their critical analysis. This sentiment is one which all sport managers should consider when looking at key events, even in the recent past, which have transformed working environments. This is particularly important in relation to risk management and analysing past accidents and tragedies.

The 1989 Hillsborough stadium tragedy offers many important points which all sport managers should consider, whether they are involved with events and stadiums or not. It offers lessons about the importance of developing a deeper understanding of management practices and the devastating results when mistakes are made, which can reverberate for years, even decades, after the event.

In 1989 at the Hillsborough football stadium, 96 football fans were crushed to death, with hundreds more injured. It is too easy to reduce the causation to operational decisions made on the day, when the gates were opened, allowing fans to pour into the ground, crushing people to death against each other and, crucially, against an immovable, tall fence with turned spiked tops.

Why did this happen and who was to blame? One of the most shocking revelations about Hillsborough were the failures by so many of the key stakeholders, ranging from government, club owners and the police, relating to: failures to analyse and learn from past events; failures to change their behaviour and improve safety practices; and failures to treat fans as customers of a service, not a problem to be dealt with by force and physical barriers. The result was that the risk of people being crushed to death was never a question of 'if' but always a question of 'when' such an event would take place during the 1970s and 1980s.

Before Hillsborough, hundreds of people had died and thousands injured in various stadium disasters over the past hundred years, such as at Ibrox in 1971, where 66 people died; and Burndon Park in 1946, when 33 fans were killed and hundreds injured. There was also criticism of Sheffield Wednesday, the club who own the Hillsborough stadium, suggesting that the club had failed to learn or implement any significant changes after an earlier incident in the a 1981 FA cup semi-final, where a number of fans were seriously injured. It was a warning sign, but one which was not heeded. Any good manager, just as any good historian, would ask why failures from the past were not learnt from.

Explore and analyse deeper and one soon discovers how the wider political, social and economic environmental factors shaped the tragedy. For example, the political conditions of the time were highly relevant, helping to explain why the fencing was erected in sport grounds, despite the potential risk of people being crushed to death against immovable obstacles, as the 1987 Heysal disaster illustrated, when 39 Italian fans died at the Heysel stadium in Belgium. After the Heysel tragedy, Mrs Thatcher, the UK prime minister, 'declared war against the hooligans' bringing in many measures to deal with the problems, ranging from creating physical barriers to separate fans, to football ID cards. This confrontational approach reflected very much the general politics of the time, which was more ideological divided and adversarial, and more specifically Mrs Thatcher's style of government. Sadly, it took Hillsborough for a fundamental break with the 'facility inertia' which had set in, when people attempted to learn from the past, not simply react to it. After Hillsborough and the publication of the 1990 Taylor report, it not only brought about many physical changes to stadiums (e.g. stadiums becoming all-seater), but it also saw a cultural change by the key stakeholders of how fans should be viewed, treated and managed. Hillsborough is a powerful and emotive case study to show the importance of analysing past incidents, in order to learn from them, acting as a reminder of the tragic consequences when we fail to learn from the past.

EXAMPLES TO ILLUSTRATE THE INEVITABILITY OF CHANGE AND THE SOCIAL CONSTRUCTION OF SPORTING VIEWS

To help you think more about your own values and how they may shape your approach to management, it can be worthwhile exploring some examples of how past views expressed by people were used to try and resist change in sport. Many of these examples are deliberately provocative, to illustrate our comment earlier about views which can now appear as 'racist, sexist, at best misguided, or just plain stupid'. They should in some of you instil a sense of incredulity, even anger, particularly as they would have been expressed by people who would have a great deal of authority at the time. Consider how these match up with your views and opinions:

- *Working-class people should be excluded from competing in rowing and athletics competitions as their work gives them an unfair advantage in competitions:* these arguments were used by people trying protect the idea of the sporting amateur in the nineteenth century. This was formalised with bans by sport organisations in athletics and rowing of dock workers (as some rowed for a living) and labourers, as they believed their work would give them an unfair advantage in amateur competitions (Henry 1993, p. 11; Mallon and Buchanan 2006, p. cii; Collins 2013, p.31). In effect this meant that only the middle-class and 'leisured' elite would be entitled to participate in competitive sport competitions until these rules were changed in the 1860s.
- *Amateurs and professional players of the same team should be segregated and treated differently:* in cricket, the Marylebone Cricket Club (MCC) insisted on having different forms of address, changing rooms and even entrances for the paid, professional players (often working class in background) and the more highly regarded amateurs (often from more privileged backgrounds), even though they were on the same team. These distinctions lasted until the 1950s, when Len Hutton, the first professional cricketer (i.e. he received a regular income for playing), was appointed as England captain.
- *Women playing sport can potentially make them infertile, overtly sexualised and masculine:* these arguments were often expressed in order to justify why women should be excluded from sport. Paradoxically, whilst for men, the playing of sport was viewed as a way of reducing 'sexuality', for women it was viewed as potentially making them more promiscuous. It reflected a belief that sport was seen as a masculine activity which can still resonate today, as illustrated by FIFA president Sepp Blatter's suggestion

that to help grow the women's game, they should 'play in different and more feminine garb than the men, in tighter shorts for example' (BBC Sport 2011). This illustrates a long history of sexism which has run through many governing bodies of sport.

• *Women should be banned from playing on FA-affiliated pitches as they should be encouraged to return to domestic home life and duties:* the English Football Association (FA) ruling of 1921, banned women from playing football on any FA-affiliated pitch, despite some women's games attracting thousands of spectators during the First World War. Women's teams were forced to find other venues in a move that put back the development of women's football for decades. The ruling was not rescinded until 1971, with the FA finally recognising women's football in 1993. To give a sense of the impact, in 1920, a year before the ban, the Dick Kerr Ladies football team played St Helen's women's team and was watched by 53,000 people; it would not be until 74 years later in 2014 when this record would be beaten, when 55,000 people attended the women's England vs Germany game at Wembley.

• *Hacking players and robust physical challenges are an important part of the game of football. Removing them would reduce the character-building elements and lessen enjoyment:* this was the view expressed by some to resist rule changes in football, whereby they believed hacking and bringing down players in football was one of the elements of the game which helped develop courage and made the game more exciting.

Most of these examples have no scientific basis. They reflect subjective and cultural bias, or simply just plain guesswork. They illustrate how people can develop views to justify why changes should be resisted. For you, the simple question to ask yourself is 'how will some of my current views about sport appear to others in the future?' Will you be seen as one leading the vanguard for change, or hopelessly out of touch with the many political, economic, social and technological changes which have taken place?

HISTORICAL OVERVIEW

Sometimes sport organisations will endeavour to find the earliest links and references to a sport, in some misguided belief that by showing its age, it can somehow give greater value and worth to a sport. These links are often spurious and distract from key historical periods when a sport was formed. In this section we give a very broad sweep of the history of sport, with the prime focus on the periods of industrialisation, colonialism and post-industrialism. Although other historical periods are important, such as the influence of ancient Greek and Roman philosophical ideas on the development of nineteenth-century British sport, there simply is not the scope to discuss these various periods in this book.

The historical development of sport can be represented in many ways. Beech and Chadwick (2004, p. 7) primarily focus on the development of commercial, professional sport, which they identify as going through seven key phases, these being:

1 *foundation*: evolution of sport activities from ancient folk games;
2 *codification* of rules of games: rules for how to play the game are established;
3 *stratification*: as sport grows, governing bodies are established to codify and enforce the rules;
4 *professionalisation*: people receive money to play a sport, which continues to be played alongside the unpaid amateurs;
5 *post-professionalisation*: proper pay structures and professional leagues established;
6 *commercialisation*: more money gained from commercial enterprises, such as the development of sponsorship; and
7 *post-commercialisation*: this is a future phase, where major revenues are received outside of sport.

In addition, these different phases can be classed as revolutionary (i.e. radical, wholesale change, such as the development of a single set of coherent rules), whilst others are evolutionary (i.e. minor changes to the sport, such as rule modifications).

Whilst this offers a very useful categorisation for the historical development of sport, in this book there is need to understand sport beyond just the commercial sector to which Beech and Chadwick (2004) restrict their analysis. It is therefore important to identify some of the broader, classic historical phases often used in textbooks to discuss both sport and leisure, with which Beech and Chadwick (2004) categorisation can then fit into. In Table 2.1 a simple summary is given of some very broad time periods, highlighting some of the key points relating to sport for those periods. Of particular importance is to recognise how certain cultural and philosophical legacies can still resonate today, along with the importance of Britain in the early stages of many sports developing around the world.

There is not the scope in this book to discuss all these key phases, so we have limited the discussion to the periods of industrialisation, colonialism and post-war developments. It should also be noted that Britain is given particular attention because, as Roberts (2004) observed, modern sport has become amongst the country's most successful exports. Of course, originating something does not necessarily mean that any special advantage or ownership will be retained, rather it simply shows where many sports began and how different cultures and economic systems will shape sport to fit their own needs, and how the technologies of the time influence the expansion and development.

IMPACT OF INDUSTRIALISATION ON SPORT

Industrialisation refers to the change in an economic system, where the manufacturing of goods becomes the dominant part of the economy. Historically, wealth was based on land and agriculture, but with industrialisation it became based in factories and, put simply, making things. This shift from agriculture to industry had profound social and political impacts, with technological innovations (such as the development of steam power) being a key driver of change. In political terms, industrial economies increasingly needed government intervention to help regulate the economy, as unfettered free-

Table 2.1   Overview of the key time periods and the implications for the development of sport

---

Ancient world

Leisure is considered in philosophical terms, whereby not everyone in society is viewed as capable of proper leisure, as it was the preserve of the elite and an elevating practice. The ancient philosophical writings of Plato and Aristotle help shape attitudes to sport and leisure in the nineteenth century, when their writings are reinvented to suit new times. The Olympic games first take place, which is again re-invented in the late nineteenth and early twentieth centuries. Romans' use of 'bread and circuses', which means people are fed and entertained in exchange for giving up political rights and supporting the emperors is also another relevant theme where sport can still be used as a means of social control by governments around the world. Play and recreation is used by the Romans as fitness for war, with this more utilitarian use of sport contrasting with the Greeks.

Medieval and renaissance world

Sport is still not a coherent concept in the early phases of this very broad time period. Many games are marked by their rarity, taking place only on certain days, such as holy days. Leisure is viewed as something which the aristocracy can use in their development of wisdom. A protestant work ethic also develops which views leisure as potentially a problem. Some sports, rooted in rural communities, begin to be more clearly established, such as boxing, racing and cricket.In the early stages, games are for either war, exhibition of wealth and power, or simply diversion. Little is to be gained by using sport as a commercial, lucrative activity. It was also more ad hoc and less organised. Sport has a very different connotation in later periods, referring to landed gentry and activities such as hunting (Horne et al 2013, p. xv), not the playing of gamses or athletic individuals.

Industrialisation 1750s to 1940s

Sport is transformed by the industrialisation process. Urbanisation and the expansion of cities creates huge audiences for various entertainments, that includes sport, which can be tapped into for commercial gain; public schools see sport as virtuous, civilising and character building. Technology, from the train, to news print, helps to further expand sport. The media in particular develops a symbiotic relationship, where sport helps sells papers, and papers help popularise sport. A relationship which has continued, but with different mediums such as satellite TV. It illustrates how sport needs a capitalist economic system in order to be more clearly defined and to expand.

Post-war 1945 to 1970s

There is greater acceptance about the role of governments to both support sport and encourage people to participate. A huge expansion in the public sector, primarily by local government, takes place in the development of sport facilities. Sport is also increasingly seen as part of welfare structures in many countries. Also global economic and political changes have continued to transform sport.

Post-industrial economy 1970s to present
Some key political shifts in capitalist economies mean new social and economic policies are developed which have profound implications for the provision of sport. There is a shift in thinking whereby there is belief in the free market to make services more efficient, such as contracting out of numerous public services, from cleaning, catering and later leisure and sport. The voluntary sector, always important, has continued to grow in order to deal with both market and government failures in the provision of sport (see Chapter 6). Sport continues to be shaped by global economic and political forces. A frequent rationale used to justify government spending on sport can be based on the notion of sport externalities (i.e. the spin off effects, such as the potential to improve health).

---

market economics led to many problems, such as political instability generated by inequalities, poor worker conditions and disease. In social terms, it also sees a shift in populations, where people move from the countryside, to concentrate in large urban environments to serve the needs of the factories making goods. People's lives are no longer task-orientated (i.e. you work until the job is done, such as ploughing a field), instead becoming time-orientated (i.e. work is done according to the clock and the hours required to work).

There has been a long running debate by historians as to the extent that the working class benefited from the industrial revolution. It is a split which has run along the fault lines of politics, with left-wing (Marxist) tending to be critical of the process, whilst more liberal commentators say that it was beneficial for the working class. A summary of the two positions involved is presented in Table 2.2, which gives a sense of how history can be different, depending on your political viewpoint.

The debate about the extent the working class benefited from the industrialisation process illustrates how malleable the past can be and why history is more than the mere recording of past incidents. It involves critical investigation, analysis and even speculation. However, there are still some broad areas where agreement appears (even if they do disagree as to the reasons for the changes, or what the ultimate outcome was). Although Clarke and Critcher (1988, p.46) broadly examine history through a Marxist perspective, they make some very pertinent and relevant observations which other non-Marxist historians would agree on. They argue that leisure today,

Table 2.2 The historical controversy of how much the working class benefited by the industrial revolution

Marxist/neo-Marxist historical position	Liberalist/pluralist historical position
Key principles: Karl Marx, writing in the nineteenth century, viewed history as a conflict between classes, which in the nineteenth and twentieth centuries is primarily between the working class majority (the proletariat) and the smaller middle class (the bourgeoisie). The argument goes that the ruling elite own the factors of production (e.g. factories, machines, etc.) and exploit workers for greater profits and self-interest. In theory, Marx predicted that the working class would revolt and set up a new society called communism.	**Key principles:** people are free to choose what they want to buy, where the market is the best mechanism for the distribution of resources. Society is not made of just two key classes, but many different competing groups. Yes, there are inequalities, but so too are there opportunities for self-improvement. For liberalists, whilst they accept that there is a great deal of exploitation, what they also point to is how conditions and pay steadily improved for workers.
View on sport: initially, when Marx was writing, he described religion as the 'opiate of the people' (it eases the pain of a tough working life now, to gain a better life in heaven); later neo-Marxist writers would describe leisure (to include sport) as the new opiate of the people, which dulls the pain and distracts them from their exploitation. Sport, education and religion are seen as tools of social control (aspects of the Roman 'circuses' here). Marxist historians are particularly critical of how the working class have many of their old pastimes destroyed, to be replaced by activities that the middle class deem as more appropriated. A simple example sometimes used to illustrate the class divisions is how working class activities involving cruelty to animals is banned, whilst foxhunting remains. The expansion of leisure and sport is also viewed as another way that the working class are exploited by commercial businesses.	**View of sport:** sport is not forced on the working class, but flourishes, where they decide what they want to watch and play. Sport and leisure activities which are not popular fail, such as alcohol-free pubs introduced but temperance movements. Whilst many old recreational pastimes are banned, such as activities involving animal cruelty, this should not be romanticized or seen as a bad thing. This is part of the 'civilising process' which is good for society (Henry 1992, p. 10). As Collins argues (2013, p. 15) the decline and disappearance of many traditional games was not due to their intrinsic qualities as games but because of changes in the world which provided their context. Also, expansion of Sunday schools, the development of public parks and mechanic institutions improved the quality of life and offered opportunities for self-improvement. Eventually, whilst the century begins by destroying leisure activities, it finishes by a huge expansion offering greater choice.

bears more resemblance with 1880, than 1880 did with 1780. They argue that the industrial revolution begins by destroying working-class leisure, not creating it (the extent this was good or bad and who actually benefited most is what the two camps disagree on). It is possible to adapt both Marxist and pluralist writers' work in order to identify some of the key changes which occur during this period, whereby sport and leisure became:

- *Specialised:* many old play and recreational spaces would be lost to the expanding urban environments, later being replaced at the end of the nineteenth century by spaces designated for a specific purpose, such as for football, athletics or cricket. A clearer demarcation is established between work and leisure, and the specialised, professional player.
- *Institutional:* many old, often chaotic pastimes would be lost, sometimes forcibly repressed. In their place are new, prescribed, leisure and sport activities, which are deemed as good for both mind and body. There is a more coherent set of philosophical ideals about sport within the private schools. Sport is given a moral purpose, which others would take and use as a tool to change and shape working-class culture, and pastimes, to try and ensure they were more industrious, good citizens.
- *Segregated:* leisure is segregated in terms of class and gender. For example, the game of football, although originally a game founded in the British universities played by the aristocracy and the middle class, eventually becomes the sport of the working class, although in terms of governance, the old ruling elites maintain control. In terms of gender, it is particularly striking how the watching and the playing of sport would become 'distinctly masculine' (Horne *et al.* 2013, p. 31). Sport for women during this time, tends to be something only middle-class women have an opportunity to participate in, focusing on a relatively narrow range of sports (e.g. golf, badminton and tennis).
- *Standardisation:* Roberts (2004, p. 84) argues that one of the more modern features about sport to develop at this time is

that it enables all classes, nationalities, religions and races to compete on equal terms as the rules have been codified and made standard, such as the development of the Queensbury rules for boxing.

- *Sporting ideologies:* private, independent schools play a pivotal role in developing many important ideas about sport, where it becomes not something just for diversion, but an activity which transforms and improves people. Teachers, imbued and soaked in the classics (i.e. the study of ancient Greece and Rome), often created a romantic and idealised picture of these ancient civilisations, wanting to recreate many of the virtues, with sport steadily gaining an elevated status as to its benefits. It is worth mentioning the three key stands which formed the foundation of a broad sport ideology here. Some of these still resonate in attitudes and philosophies about sport today, around the world which are:
  - *Amateurism:* the idea that sport should not be played for material reward, playing for the love of the game, or for its own sake. It embodied ideas of fair play and to lose and triumph with grace, and, even more loftily, to unite humanity through its enjoyment.
  - *Rational recreation:* a view of sport believed by various disparate philanthropic and church groups, who were concerned with the moral welfare of the urban working class, seeking to provide more 'wholesome' alternatives to pre-industrial leisure forms.
  - *Muscular Christianity:* part of this broad movement, which focused on promoting the newly codified sports games into working-class communities, which they believed would help foster the virtues of self-discipline, deferred gratification, teamwork and the subordination of individual interests to the greater collective good.
  - *Commercialisation:* during this period it becomes possible to make sport a profitable commercial activity. Before industrialisation sport and games were more sporadic, offering some opportunities for paying spectators or gambling, now the geographic concentration of people, along with and the desire for entrainment meant many

market opportunities were created. Roberts (2004) offers the interesting argument that it is the commercial sector which was more effective at opening up sport, rather than the amateur governing bodies of sport, which were hemmed in by their narrow ideological commitment to notions of amateurism.

When exploring these changes, it is important to remind you that it is the changing political, economic, social and technological forces (PEST factors) which are driving change, constantly creating opportunities and threats for sport organisations. Identifying these changes and considering the risks they generate for sport organisations is a remarkably similar process to what contemporary managers have to do when making strategic plans, as will be explained in Chapter 4.

COLONIALISM

The combination of Britain being the first country to industrialise and the scale of its empire are key to understanding how sports invented in Britain spread around the world. Colonialism refers to an exploitative, acquisition process, which can be characterised by the following points:

- securing raw materials/secure markets;
- acquisition of territory/space/land which is colonised;
- mercantilism (governments control foreign trade);
- varies in terms of the scale of the settlements (i.e. plantation colonies);
- introduce political and social structures to rule;
- these structures can be used to separate/distinguish between colonisers and indigenous groups, or used to inculcate other groups used for ruling.

Understanding how sport is used in colonialism and the growth in international trade gives insights into how certain sports become established around the world. Have you ever wondered why cricket is the most important sport in India, Pakistan, or why football is the number one game in South

America? Exploring the history reveals that in relation to South America, it was the weakness of colonialism, but the strength of trade, along with the work of middle-class engineers and workers from Britain who went to South America who helped introduce the game to the countries, with their influence also helping to explain why Argentina is one of the few South American countries which plays rugby. For colonised countries, the maintenance of such a huge empire, by such a small country, was difficult and whilst the use of military force (hard power) gives part of the answer of how it managed to do this, the other more subtle means to maintain control came through the use of soft power, such as education and sport. Britain would use the soft power of sport in an instrumental way to help justify and maintain its rule. Initially, the playing of sports by the British colonisers was not only a way of maintaining cultural links with the home country, but it also helped segregate and differentiate themselves from the indigenous populations, helping to prove to themselves that they were more civilised and superior, and so had a right to rule. Later, as schools were set up in these countries the training of local people to become part of the established ruling elite became important, with the ideas and values of sport developed in British public schools being replicated in these schools. Furthermore, the growth in tours by cricket and rugby teams, particularly to Australia and South Africa, offered a further means to maintain the cultural links with Britain. We still see this today with the Lions rugby tour and the Ashes test matches in cricket.

The sporting culture which is developed in the nineteenth century as part of colonialism is a highly racialised one, which can still resonate today. In the past simplistic, stereotypical attitudes developed of the white, gentlemen colonisers characterised by their control, cool-headedness, emotional restraint, whilst the indigenous populations, were often portrayed as more physical, emotional and instinctive, but lacking discipline (Crabbe and Wagg 2000). These are now rightly regarded as ludicrously anachronistic, used to justify political rule, having no scientific foundation; yet where these attitudes can still creep into the reporting and governance of sport. The irony is that although sport was used to maintain colonial rule, it could also be turned against the colonial masters, as it is used create and reforge new cultural identities (Crabbe and Wagg 2000) which would help break with colonialism

POST-WAR PROVISION

The end of the Second World War was transformative in politics around the world. For liberal capitalist economies, from the USA to the UK, there was an expectation that governments should intervene in the economy to ensure economic growth and keep unemployment low. The importance of the principle of intervention is a vital one and whilst initially it has a modest effect on sport, it later becomes crucial (see Chapter 6 for an explanation of the economic mix).

In the UK and many European countries, more coherent welfare structures were established. This meant that the state provided healthcare, education and a safety net of payments for people who become unemployed, rather than people having to rely on charitable donations. It is not until the 1960s that more coherent policies are developed for the provision of sport and leisure, when there was recognition of the importance of sport to individuals, society and the economy and that governments should support this. Provision and support for sport came through the establishment of the Sport Council in 1965. This and other agencies used government money to establish the delivery of sport and leisure. The impetus for setting up this council was given by the 1960 Wolfenden Report, which gave the rationale for state involvement not necessarily because of sport's intrinsic worth (i.e. it is something which gives enjoyment), but because of extrinsic factors, such as Britain's failing reputation in international sport competition, along with how sport could be used to deal with many youth subcultures which were seen as more morally dubious (Henry 1993, p. 17).

In the UK, local government began to play a more direct role in the provision of sport by building more sport facilities In 1972, there were 30 municipal (i.e. owned by local government) sport centres, and 500 indoor swimming pools; by 1978 this had increased to 350 sport centres and more than 850 pools (Henry 1993, p. 22) – clear evidence of the new intervention and funding.

Up until the 1980s there was a great deal of political agreement around sport and leisure particularly around the value and role of sport. The ideas that people can be 'recreationally deprived' and that people had a right to leisure, which included sport, became a key belief. Indeed as the 1975 government white paper on sport and recreation (DoE 1975) stated, 'sport and recreation is part of the social fabric'. It meant, as Coalter (1990) notes, that sport and leisure should be provided as part of broader welfare provision, such as with health or education.

The commercial sector continued to grow. New technological innovations, such as the growth of TV and broadcasting, and a growing practice of commercial sponsorship, fuelled spending. Rapid growth was also found in the USA transforming the provision of sport, while in other countries and sport organisations, there was much slower progress to adapt to the many commercial opportunities on offer. Commercialisation would become a key driver of change, which many would resist, but not actually stop.

SPORT IN THE POST-INDUSTRIAL ECONOMY

We refer here to how the economies have shifted, from the old traditional forms of manufacturing and mineral extraction, to high-quality manufactured goods and services. In the West this also meant that the manufacturing of goods moved to other countries, particularly China, to benefit from lower costs. The German tennis manufacturer, Head, illustrates how these global economic changes work in practice with their operations now split between two countries. The mass-produced racquets for more mainstream markets are manufactured in China, while the organisation's HQ is based in the small Austrian town of Kennelbach, which focuses on the niche, top end of the market and custom building racquets to the design specifications of the customer or the tennis players they sponsor, such as Novak Djokovic (Lee 2015).

These structural shifts began in the 1970s, but with some of the biggest and quickest changes occurring in the 1980s when the new economic policies of monetarism began to take hold on governments around the world. Indeed, one of the key shifts during the 1980s was a shift back to older, liberal economic policies, where there was greater emphasis on the role of the free market, with a call for governments to intervene less in the economy.

The debate about which sector is best to deliver sport provision and how much governments should intervene has continued to go through ebbs and flows, but what has been evident is that there has been a blurring between the public, voluntary and commercial sectors. As governments around the world are under pressure to control debts, they have increasingly sought the voluntary and private sector to fill the gaps. In turn, the voluntary sector has had to think more carefully about being efficient with resources and how to generate revenues. Finally, the commercial sector has had to consider issues of ethics and how they can be a responsible organisations which can protect environments and people's human rights. Sport, since the 1980s, has continued to grow and become more commercial, with huge amounts of money available to some (just think about how much broadcasters now pay to show live sporting events). Sport has continued to be professionalised and to succeed at the top level there is a need for significant resources and commitment. Interestingly this commitment will often come from a mixture of money from the commercial sector or government funds because sport stars are an increasingly important part of our society that can influence behaviour and stimulate participation in sport and physical activity.

The other crucial implication of these shifts has been to see the rapid rise of new economies, which have been crucial in generating economic growth around the world. These current global shifts are vital to understand, so we will return to them in Chapter 6, when we explore globalisation.

GLOBALISATION AND NEW MARKETS –
THE CASE OF CRICKET

The development of global expansion of cricket offers many interesting examples of how sport has been shaped by industrialisation, colonialism and some of the current global shifts. Initially, Gemmell (2011, p. 707) argues that cricket was viewed as one of the means of securing the legitimacy and ethos of the British Empire. It was played in the schools, encouraged by local officials and became a component of cultural capital. But, by the end of the nineteenth century, cricket in India and the West Indies, was more about enforcing a set of structural values that encapsulated Englishness amid the fear of the white population 'going native'. A number of interesting observations can be made about cricket and colonialism in relation to a number of countries, such as:

- *India:* cricket in India is an important part of the social fabric, which permeates into politics, culture and religion, with cricket players adored (Nair 2011). In India, as the popularity of cricket grew, the sport was initially used to maintain divisions, such as basing teams on religious groupings, in a divide and rule policy. The economic power of cricket has shifted from the likes of England and Australia, and is now firmly set in India, with TV audiences for big one day internationals hitting 200 million in 2011 and some reaching upwards of 400 million (a fifth of the population) (Nair 2011, p. 270). In addition, the amount of money which has flown into the new IPL league since its inception has been staggering, with some estimates that it has been around $2 billion.
- *Australia:* sport in general and cricket in particular became an important focus for developing national identity, with the baggy green cap worn by the cricketers becoming a potent national symbol of Australian nationalism, even though it is one wrapped up in a great deal of invented tradition (Croke and Harper 2011). It is one which has powerful marketing properties, which Australian cricket have long recognised and noted in various strategic plans, whereby they try to foster 'seemingly organic and enduring connection'

between Australian cultural identity and cricket, which has some powerful marketing and commercial opportunities (Croke and Harper 2011). This also shows the value of understanding the heritage of a sport from a business position.

- *West Indies and the Caribbean:* C. L. R. James was a Caribbean-born writer who wrote a number of seminal texts on cricket, sport and colonialism. In his 1963 book, *Beyond a Boundary,* he looks at cricket through its social and political dimensions, using a Marxist perspective. Whilst he knew that sport in general, and cricket in particular, was a force for conservatism, representing segregated class and racial interests, he also considered how it could be used for more 'revolutionary' purposes to bring about change. This was represented by the fact the early West Indies cricket team were all white, with a gradual acceptance of black players, until whites were hardly represented at all. This did not stop the captain continuing to be white until Frank Worrel was appointed the first black captain. An appointment made easier for the white governing board, as Frank had a degree and had played in England. James and the West Indies were also important forces in maintaining the pressure to boycott South Africa from sport whilst it operated a system of apartheid. In the Caribbean, the once unassailable centrality of cricket, epitomised by the dominance that the West Indies teams had in the 1970s and 1980s, has found that it is competing with other sports for the hearts and minds of young people. The impact of satellite TV, the influence of the USA, has meant that sports such as basketball, with its strong cultural links with hip-hop American culture, can have more appeal.

- *South Africa:* whilst sports such as cricket have provided a mechanism for integration, in South Africa it was also very much used to maintain social segregation and political exclusion, particularly in relation to cricket and rugby. It was not really until the 1960s and 1970s that sport is used as a point of leverage to put pressure on South Africa to abolish the system of racial apartheid. The boycotts, the arguments and the case of Basil D'Olivera are excellent to illustrate the dynamics of change and how the forces of conservatism within sport try and resist change.

Looking at the historical evolution of cricket offers many interesting and relevant examples to illustrate how changes in the external business environment create the dynamics for opportunistic and threatening changes. For example, there are now three formats of the game of cricket: the five-day test game, the one-day game and the more recent Twenty20 format. There were many who resisted the Twenty20 format, being particularly concerned for how it would impact on the classic, five-day game (in fact, if anything it has far more impact on the one-day game, rather than the five-day game). The growth in this format shows how it meets a need of people who may be more cash-rich, but time poor, where they do not have the time to commit for longer formats of the game. The new format has also been very attractive to the media and satellite TV, as it lasts for approximately three hours, equivalent to an American football game.

CONCLUSION

Sport has evolved over time from something quite narrow, focusing on a small range of activities, predominantly for males, to something much broader. It now includes a wide range of activities, where there are demands to make it more inclusive. Whilst sport is often presented as a positive force for change, looking at the history gives a reminder of how it has also been a conservative force, to resist change and reinforce inequalities. It also gives insights where many of the ideas about the virtues and goodness of sport originated from, where it has become a received wisdom, which is often accepted without criticism and viewed as fact and continuously reissued by those involved in sport.

Sport managers can learn a lot from both the principles of history and the historical development of sport. In terms of learning from the historian, it is about understanding the importance of critically scrutinising the past. In terms of the actual history, it is to show how change is a constant dynamic, which must be managed and dealt with, not simply resisted. Yes there can be problems with relying too much on the past to anticipate the future, but overall, the weight of evidence is that it can do far more good than bad. It is vital that managers look at the past, but do not become lost and confined there. You need to reflect on your own values and positions to consider how they may change in the future.

Looking at the past is a key foundation for building in the future. It shows where a business, organisation or service has come from, how it has dealt with past opportunities and threats and potentially how it should deal with future opportunities and threats. Examples of people in organisations that have either embraced change, or resisted change should provide powerful reminders for you to review your thinking, attitudes and organisational culture. When dealing with an issue, just think back to the people who fought against the narrow, white, male, middle-class elites who ran many sports, who believed that those who played the sport should be a simple reflection of those who run the sport. Now, the arguments put forward by many who would have been deemed 'experts' of their day, can seem quite breathtaking in the levels of racism, sexism, or just simply ignorance that these views reflect. It should remind us that our cultural values and beliefs are subjective and ever changing.

3

ORGANISATIONAL THEORY AND THE FUNCTIONS, SKILLS AND ROLES OF MANAGEMENT

INTRODUCTION

This chapter has been designed to give you a brief overview of some of the key, classic theories about organisations and management. We pay particular attention to examining the functions, roles and skills that you, as a manager of *any* organisation, would need to consider. Particular attention is given to the key skills of time management, motivation, communication and leadership: vital skills for a manager in any business, let alone a sporting one. As usual we'll also provide a number of sport-related examples so that you can see how things work in practice. Finally, we'll look at the importance of transferable skills which can be used in the sport industry and beyond, should you choose a career in the mainstream business sector.

DEVELOPMENT OF ORGANISATIONAL THEORY AND HUMAN RESOURCE MANAGEMENT

The history of management theory is intimately tied to the study of organisations. Indeed, Follet's (1918) commonly cited definition of management of 'getting things done through other people' is founded on the principle that these 'people' are part of an organisation which needs to be managed. This has meant that a critical part of the research, analysis and development of theories about management have focused on how organisations work and can be made more productive. If we accept that organisations are, in essence, about bringing groups of people together to achieve some goal or objective, it is not surprising that a good part of organisational theory focuses on the people within the organisation and how managers can lead and motivate teams of people. It is also from this field of study that the management function of human resource management (HRM) (something that we will return to in Chapter 4) has developed, referring specifically to the management of people so that we can improve individual performance and effectiveness, for the achievement of the organisation's operational and strategic objectives (see Chapter 5 for an explanation of these levels).

People form organisations for differing purposes, ranging from making a profit, strengthening community cohesion, increasing participation and so on. Understanding the purpose is important for a variety of reasons, ranging from: classifying an organisation's legal identity; regulatory and governance rules; and eligibility to apply for grants, donations and tax concessions. Indeed, it can be quite surprising just how many ways an organisation can be categorised for legal and regulatory purposes. Just in the UK this includes: association; trust; partnership; company limited by guarantee; company limited by shares; industrial and provident society; limited liability partnership; community interest company limited by guarantee; community interest company limited by shares; and charitable incorporated organisation (Governance Hub and Cooperatives UK 2009). Similar categorisations can be found in many other countries.

In Figures 3.1 and 3.2 we've provided two simplified examples of organisational structures which focus on the key senior management roles. The first relates to Sydney University Sports and Fitness, which is classified as a charitable enterprise. They operate the sport services for

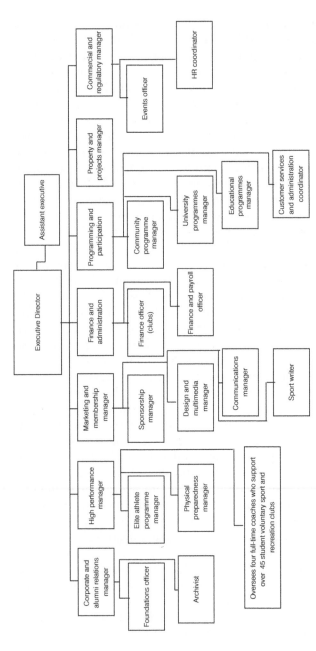

Figure 3.1 Organisational structure and management positions for a charity classified sport organisation (adapted from Sydney University Sport and Fitness 2014)

the University of Sydney and although it has its roots as a voluntary association based around the university, students' union and societies, it now operates as a separate, professional organisation. In terms of its legal organisational status, it is a registered charity, which means it will need to comply to a variety of regulations relating to charities, such as what it can do with any money raised through commercial activities, fund raising or tax-free donations. In terms of the organisation's key remit, it has developed a broad variety of functions, ranging from managing the university sport facilities and supporting around 45 different voluntary sport and recreation clubs, for both general recreation and elite athlete development. Looking at the organisational hierarchical structure in Figure 3.1, it's interesting to note how it has a mixture of traditional functional roles, relating to finance and marketing (discussed in Chapter 4), to more specialised functions, such as those relating to the corporate and alumni manager.

The second example (Figure 3.2) gives you a (simplified) diagram of the senior management structure for the sport manufacturer Nike. You'll probably know that Nike is a huge global business that employs thousands of people around the world – and sells lots of sport apparel. What you might not know is that in terms of its legal status, it is classified as a public limited company (PLC – basically an organisation that sells chunks of itself on a stock exchange so investors can make money from their shares if the organisation does well or lose money if it does badly). To give you a sense of scale of its operations and the number of management jobs that would be needed, it's worth noting that when Nike unveiled their strategy during an investors meeting in 2010, their key revenue target was $27 billion by the end of 2015 (Nike 2010). To achieve this involves developing a clear strategic plan (see Chapter 5), which is then steadily devolved down through managers at different levels of the hierarchy, until it gets to the operational level, where, for example, a sales manager may have monthly targets to try to hit. Take a look at the structure. What is of interest to note here is how there is a mixture of roles based around traditional business functions (discussed in Chapter 4), such

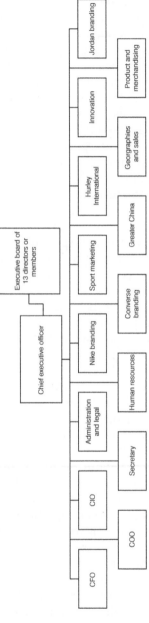

Figure 3.2 Simplified senior management structure for Nike (adapted from Nike 2014)

as the marketing and HR roles, to more specific roles, which focus on specific brands, such as Converse, or key markets, such as the one relating to Asia.

When we examine organisational structures and the management within them, there is a rich body of literature which challenges the traditional, top-down hierarchical stance many organisations adopt, particularly for large corporations. Handy (1985) notes how a silo mentality (i.e. you only think about your own job or department) could develop in large organisations, which can lead to goals becoming confused: that is to say that the job or task in hand is seen as more important than the overall reason of why it is done, or people failing to appreciate other people's work. Another example relates to Peter's work in 1986 (cited in Wolsey 2011, p. 360) and his theory about inverting the organisational pyramid, so that it is characterised by senior staff supporting junior staff at the point of customer delivery (it can be good when the bosses get their hands dirty). Think for a moment about how this approach would look in our two examples of organisations, whereby the senior executive position are placed at the bottom and the hierarchy expanded and mapped out to all the front line operational jobs.

FUNCTIONS, SKILLS AND ROLES OF MANAGEMENT

In terms of management, Henry Fayol published his book *The Principles of Management*, way back in 1916 and laid a critical foundation for the scientific study of management and organisations. This work identified five key functions of management, which are still commonly referred to in many books on management today. These five functions were introduced in Chapter 1, with the 'command' function adjusted to 'communicate' and are summarised in Table 3.1. Fayol also described fourteen *principles* of management, which will not be discussed here, but are mentioned so that you can appreciate the difference between the use of the term *functions* and *principles*.

As the applied science of management and organisational theory has developed, so too have the attempts to further clarify what the essence of management is. For example, Mintzberg's work in the 1960s identified and elaborated on the different set of inter-related roles and behaviours which managers needed to adopt. In all, ten key roles were identified, organised into three key categories of: interpersonal, informational and decisional roles, again explained in Table 3.1. Whilst giving some useful elaborations on what managers

Table 3.1   Summarising management functions, roles and skills

Fayol's functions of management	Mintzberg's roles of management	Katz's skills of management
Planning (goal setting, timescales, deadlines, milestones) **Organising** (who does what, when, where and how) **Leading** (giving direction, energising, motivating, building teams) **Controlling** (supervising, tracking, reviewing, monitoring) **Communicating** (adapts the old command function and relates to informing people what has to be done, listening, adapting etc.)	**Interpersonal roles:** • Figurehead (ceremonial, awards etc.) • Leader (disciplining, training, motivation) • Liaison (contacting and communicating with other groups, developing networks) **Informational roles:** • Monitor (scrutinises different information) • Disseminator (tells others about plans, actions, policies etc.) • Spokesperson (analyses and presents the information, giving opinion and comment on it) **Decisional roles:** • Entrepreneur (new ideas, analysing business environment) • Disturbance handler (sorting out problems, making decisions) • Resource allocator (assigning project funding and resources) • Negotiator (representing organisation at key meetings)	**Technical skills** (the ability to apply specialised knowledge or expertise) **Human skills** (the ability to work and motivate others, understand needs. Now more refined such as the area of emotional intelligence) **Conceptual skills** (identify problems, have the capacity to analyse, reflect and learn from problems and adapt to situations) The mix would relate to the extent that they would be defined as a supervisor, bureaucrat or a true manager.

need to do, they are perhaps too focused on large American manufacturing corporations on which his work was primarily based (Mintzberg 1989).

The skills of management are even more important when we consider the practicalities of management. In terms of these skills, Katz's commonly cited three key management skills (Katz and Kahn 1978) presented in Table 3.1, can be very helpful (based around technical skills, human skills and conceptual skills, cited in Robbins and Judge 2012 p. 42).

It is easy to find other examples of how management can be described and categorised in relation to what they are there for and need to do. For example, Masteralixis and colleagues in their book on sport management, say:

> The goal of managerial work and the role the manager plays within an organisation is to get the workers to do what the manager wants them to do, in an efficient and cost-effective manner.
>
> (Masteralixis *et al.* 2005, p. 20)

They go on to say that this managerial work is performed through a managerial 'process' (not function) which involves planning, organising, leading and evaluating. The use of the different terms of management *functions, roles and processes* may be initially confusing, but what is important is to recognise that they are in essence giving a description of *what* managers should be doing. What they don't do though is give much insight into *how* these functions and roles should actually be done. *How* managers should perform the functions and *when* they do so, begins to move closer to the actual practicalities of management.

Into this mix of functions, roles and skills goes the need to balance and reconcile the needs of the organisation, the needs of the group and the needs of the individual. Whilst in many instances they will overlap, at times they can also conflict with each other, creating points of tension which a manager must deal with. By way of a simplistic example, think about the implications of employees working beyond their allocated hours in order to complete a task from an organisation's point of view. Yes, it can save the organisation money, which may

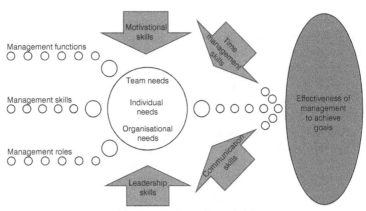

Figure 3.3   An overview of functions, roles, styles and skills

work in the short term, but in the longer term it may not be healthy for the individual, team or their motivation to work extended hours without pay.

To help illustrate the relationship of all these elements, Figure 3.3 gives an overview of how the functions, roles and skills link together. We show here an example where a manager is trying to coordinate and control many different elements, some of which can pull them in different directions. To carry out the management functions is to engage with the management process, where you can use various management skills to reconcile conflicts and tensions. Initially, when organisations and management began to be studied more systematically, there was a belief that a scientific, rational approach could be taken, whereby the organisation was almost seen as something mechanical, where all the key component parts could be examined to understand how they work. As the subject field of organisational and management theory has developed, whilst the scientific approach is still there, management now tends to be seen more as an art, rather than a precise science (Torkildsen 2005, p. 370), where managers often have to make decisions based on judgements rather than precise mathematical formulae.

KEY THEORIES IN EFFECTIVE MANAGEMENT OF ORGANISATIONS

By different functions, roles and skills we describe what a manager needs to do and how they should do it. Recognising and understanding these different areas can aid reflection on personal strengths and weaknesses, which can then help identify areas for training and development. To further enable your reflection process and to consider how the skills of management can be further refined, it can be useful to explore a number of other key concepts and theories which can help any manager more skilfully conduct their functions and roles. This will help to achieve organisational aims and objectives and are broadly based around:

- *personal skills:* time management, task analysis and delegation;
- *human skills:* relating to motivation, communication and leadership.

When you consider these different elements, do appreciate how they can blend in with the different skills of management. If staff are not motivated to complete a task effectively, then this will need an analysis of the situation (conceptual skills), drawing on both an intuitive and theoretical understanding of what motivates people (human skills and potentially technical skills). The measures which may be put in place by the manager to try and improve staff motivation, will depend on the quality of the analysis (i.e. did they identify and analyse the key factors causing the problems) and how they implement them, such as how the manager communicates to staff any changes or new initiatives. The belief and confidence of any new policies that staff or team members have can also be dependent on the leadership qualities of the manager.

PERSONAL SKILLS: TIME MANAGEMENT, TASK ANALYSIS AND DELEGATION

A critical element for performing any management functions is to be able to analyse, prioritise and delegate work effectively.

Table 3.2   Simplified job tasks checklist for a new sport programme

Initial broad job tasks identified

Market research
- Reading trade journals and marketing reports
- Informal focus groups with non-users (who interviews, where, when etc.)
- Questionnaire (who designs? interviewed or online? data analysed, etc.)

Costing and pricing
- Calculation of numbers
- All costs identified (staffing, energy, marketing, equipment etc.)
- Comparisons with competitors, etc.

Staffing
- Checking staff and coaching qualifications
- Checking coaches' and instructors' availability
- Identifying staffing needs (costing, booking, timing before activity starts, etc.)

Marketing
- Designing posters and leaflets, in-house or out-house organisations, checking of proofs, distribution lists, etc.
- Writing press releases,
- Designing online campaigns, social media etc.

This will often mean a manager being able to look at a job, have the capacity to break the job into the different tasks and to execute instructions. Table 3.2 gives a simple example of some of the job tasks which may be involved if a manager was given the task of developing a new fitness programme or coaching class at a sport facility. To complete this task effectively, it has to be broken up into the individual job tasks which need to be completed if it is to be successful. This can involve doing some preliminary (feasibility) analysis for the programme through some market research or costing analysis of the programme. The list in Table 3.2, may seem obvious, but it has a deceptive simplicity to it. Take for example the staffing task. The programme may be able to be done with existing staff, but if this is not possible, consideration may need to be given to training existing staff, or bringing in outside casual, qualified staff to deliver the programme. The manager might also consider if it is possible to delegate any of this work.

If you go through each of the tasks highlighted in Table 3.2, you'll begin to appreciate that they, depending on the scale and complexity of the programme, can represent many hours or days of work. Once a sense of the range of jobs or tasks has been identified it is time to engage with the *management functions*, which are:

- Tasks are put into a *plan*. This can be a simple action plan or checklist of tasks which identify what needs to be done, who is doing it and when it is to be completed.
- Staff and resources are *organised*. Time allocations are agreed, work is delegated and training time is identified.
- A *lead* in terms of direction is given. Staff are engaged in what has to be done, by when and by whom. This helps inspire confidence that the tasks are worthwhile.
- Information is *communicated*. Any work delegated is properly explained, people are told of dates for training, and confirmation is given of their availability.
- Tasks are *controlled*. This ensures that any work delegated is being done, deadlines are monitored, and confirmation of bookings is received.

How effectively these functions are done will depend on the skills of the manager. For example, in Figure 3.3 the skills of time management, motivation, leadership and teamwork are highlighted, which must be applied to manage or balance the conflicting needs between individuals, groups and the organisation. To do this will require a manager to effectively manage both their own and other people's time efficiently and effectively. This management of time is often overlooked in terms of its importance, but you overlook it at your peril given that time management is a critical ingredient which allows the manager to:

- keep track of delegated tasks, knowing who is doing what and by when with any work which is delegated;
- plan and allocate time to work on job tasks;
- control their work, rather than just simply reacting and working to immediate, critical deadlines.

A manager who is effective in their time management is a manager who is more likely to be seen in control of events and their time, rather than someone who is constantly reacting to events and seen as disorganised. In turn, a manager who is seen as effective with their time and completes jobs on time can enhance their leadership qualities, creating confidence in the team, which in turn can motivate them to perform better. For you, the development of time management skills will begin with your university or college work and assignments.

HUMAN SKILLS: MOTIVATION

As part of the management process to achieve organisational objectives, it should be clear that the skill of managing people is pivotal. The level of motivation or staff satisfaction an employee feels will often determine their productivity or quality of service. Essentially, motivation relates to what factors energise people or generate human actions, and has two key elements to it: what factors *energise* people to engage with an activity or task in the first instance, then what factors can *sustain* that action. This is where a manager's understanding of the basic principles of what motivates (or demotivates) people can be important. It is a theme returned to in Chapter 7, where some of the theories discussed here are reconsidered in relation to the demand and motivation to participate in sport. For now the importance of managing staff cannot be stressed enough, particularly in the large sport and leisure service sector. Wolsey says of staff in the leisure sector:

> Excellent staff are as important as excellent facilities in meeting customer requirements. Therefore, senior professionals and managers must have knowledge, experience and understanding of staff matters: staff motivation, organisational structures and the impact of these important areas on both organisation and staff performance.
>
> (Wolsey 2011, p. 340)

In various early works of organisational and management theory, often classified as having the 'scientific approach', the main focus was about improving productivity, and was founded on a relatively simplistic view of human motivation. For example, Frederick Taylor's book the *Principles of Scientific Management*, published in 1911, primarily focused on studying people in a factory setting. He examined how productivity could be increased by the technical analysis of the jobs, or time and motion studies. Simply put, time and motion studies looked at how long it took someone to complete a job, then ways were looked at to see if by changing the job, or job process, time could be saved and productivity increased. This scientific school viewed people in a dispassionate, almost mechanical way, as being simply motivated by financial rewards.

Since then, our understanding of motivation and what directs behaviour has continued to develop and move away from these old, mechanistic ways of seeing human behaviour. Instead, more attention has been given to the psychological and physiological factors which help explain what motivates people to perform certain actions, with this change sometimes described as the growth in the human relations school of thought. In Table 3.3, we've given you a summary of some of the key motivation theories to show the breadth of theories that have developed. One of the most basic theories for you to understand relates to Maslow's hierarchy of needs. In essence this takes us back to understanding basic human intrinsic (i.e. internal) needs and how this drives or motivates people to act. Whilst a little simplistic and deterministic, the value of this work when it first appeared in the 1950s was that it moved away from the simple focus on people only being motivated by money (an extrinsic, or external factor). Alderfer(1972) refined these needs (see Table 3.2), publishing his ERG (existence, relatedness, growth) theory in 1969; needs which were more easily adaptable to a work context.

McGregor published his X and Y theory in 1960 which further illustrated the changing attitudes to staff and how to motivate them. Managers who were classed as X managers had a natural suspicion and distrust of staff, believing that unless closely supervised, people would shirk work; Y managers on the other hand, placed more trust and have more confidence in people to get work done. Hertzberg, another influential writer in the human relations school, developed a theory that money was not necessarily a good motivator, but was what he called a *hygiene* factor: something which affects the degree of contentment in work, but which does not necessarily get people to work better or harder. Instead, he argued that other factors, such as personal and skill development and people having the opportunity to put these skills into practice were what really motivated people. Roberts (2004, p. 90) offers an interesting example of this theory in relation to rugby union before its professionalisation in the mid-1990s and argues that players were no less motivated or committed than the modern professional (paid) rugby union player, helping to illustrate this theory that money is an extrinsic hygiene factor, rather than an instrinsic motivator. All these theories, along with a few additional ones which can often be discussed in management books, are summarised in Table 3.3 which you can use to draw on to help analyse and design strategies to improve people's performance at work.

When considering how to motivate staff, or prevent demotivation, you should never use just one theory to help analyse their working environment. The key is to consider how the different theories can be used help analyse working environments and making informed decisions to keep staff directed and motivated. If you think back to the example about the new sport programme introduced in the previous section, these different motivational theories can be considered in relation to the staff who will engage with the activity. To begin with, a manager understanding basic needs will be able to ensure that staff feel secure in their work and that they are not over-worked. Failing to acknowledge these basic needs could lead to tired, demotivated staff, alongside

Table 3.3   Key management motivational theories

Maslow and Alderfer's need categories

Maslow's (1943) theory focuses on the need to satisfy basic needs, before progressing on to the next one. This is a basic theory, which students need to understand, even if the practical applications can be a little limited.

The hierarchy is represented as a pyramid, where; as needs become satisfied, one can move up the hierarchy to satisfy other needs, which are: 1. physiological (e.g. food, water etc.); 2. safety and security; 3. belongingness, social and love; 4. esteem; 5. self-actualisation.

Alderfer (1972) agrees with the needs but focuses only on three sets of needs: 1. existence (food, air water, pay, working conditions); 2. relatedness (meaningful social and interpersonal interactions); 3. growth (individual making creative or productive contributions).This is his ERG theory.

McGregor's (1960) X and Y theory

He identified ways that managers would view people:

X authoritarian, negative view of human nature, where people dislike work, will try to avoid it, prefer direction, or otherwise they will shirk work, therefore they need to be coerced and threatened in order to get things done. Simple adoption of the carrot (payment) or stick approach (lose job).

Y participative, positive view of human nature where work can be self-directed and self-controlled, if they are committed to the objectives, together with being able to learn and seek responsibility. It was this style of management which McGregor saw as the more positive one.

Although the types are simplistic, giving two extremes, it can still be a useful theory to understand, whereby you can do a test to see which way you tend towards. Having an awareness of your cultural view of people can in turn help in the analysis of problems and situations. His work was given further refinement by Likert (1967) who identified four management systems: 1. exploitative authoritarian; 2. benevolent authoritarian; 3 consultative; 4 participative.

Hertzberg's (1959) Two-factor theory

1. Motivators/intrinsic (get people to do things/energise and sustain motivation), such as: achievement, recognition, responsibility, growth, training and the opportunity given to be able to use it.

2. Hygiene/extrinsic factors (stop people getting unhappy), such as: salary/pay, security, nice conditions, status, procedures, etc.

The importance of his work is that he challenged the motivational properties of pay. Also, interestingly, he observed that if people are trained, then the worse thing to do is not let them use those skills they have developed. Also argued that one should not deny proper treatment of people in the beginning in the hope it can be made up later. There are problems with Hertzberg's work, whereby the validity can be challenged, but it still gives a simple analytical framework for managers to reflect on.

Other useful theories

Equity theory: Adams (1963) considers how comparisons made between the individual and others can affect their motivation, such as if they believe they put in the same amount of effort (the input), but receive different rewards (the outcome) compared with others, which can demotivate them. The crucial point is not what the actual situation may be but the perceived sense of equity, whereby it may not be the actual reward, but how it is perceived.

Expectancy theory: Vroom (1964) belief that a certain effort will lead to a certain outcome. This can influence the effort/performance balance.

Goal-directed theory – Set clear goals and outcomes to motivate staff and improve performance. It can energise them and sustain the motivation to achieve the outcome.

ABC of behaviour: this refers to Antecedent (what happens before the behaviour or action, such as how they feel, actions of others, do they know what has to be done) which causes the Behaviour (do they know what is wanted, can it be done etc.), resulting in a Consequence. The idea is that through a variety of techniques behaviour can be influenced. There are a number of variations and more sophisticated adaptions to this theory. Aspects of reinforcement theory can be relevant here (e.g. praise during the task), along with consideration to how rewards or punishments can be used.

issues of safety, as tired people are more likely to make mistakes (the 'human error' issue often cited in accidents). In order to try to *energise* people in the first instance, it can be a test of both *leadership* and *communication skills*, as you try to show why the activity is worthwhile and exciting. If you are more of a 'Y' orientation manager, your inclination is to trust staff, meaning that you have confidence in the staff to complete the tasks delegated, but using your skills in time management to periodically check that the task delegated is on track. To help with motivation further, the principles of goal theory behaviour can be used, and clear outcomes given to staff, along with recognising and praising good work. The decision taken to train staff and develop their skills can be considered in relation to Hertzberg's work, where he stressed that this is an important motivator, but if staff have been trained, they must be given an opportunity to use these new skills, otherwise they can become frustrated and demotivated. However, an awareness of equity theory means you would need to consider the implications of selecting some staff for training over others in the team. At times, if the person is failing to do the work to a satisfactory standard, constructive criticisms may be needed, even punishments.

HUMAN SKILLS: COMMUNICATIONS

One of the key attributes of a great manager is being able to communicate their decisions, organisational policies and strategies, or their analysis of a situation. Often a manager may have done some fantastic analysis of the business environment and developed a comprehensive strategy (see Chapter 5), but if it cannot be communicated to people, then that work will count for little. In terms of *who* a manager has to communicate with, these relate to the key stakeholders in the organisation or activity, which can initially be the senior managers, staff, board of governors and customers. We can extend this group, though, particularly in sport management, to include local community groups, sponsors, other sport agencies and governments (these are known as the key stakeholders). How information is communicated can also vary considerably, ranging from verbal conversations, presentations, written reports, emails, social media or the ever dependable phone call. As technology has developed, so too has the range of options that managers have to communicate with people.

Traditionally, as explored earlier, importance has been placed on having a clear organisational hierarchy, with a unity of command, often presented in a pyramid format. Information would also tend to be seen as flowing down from the top, through the organisational layers in a cascade effect. Having a dominance of single flow of communication can work to a point, reflecting a more authoritarian style, but there are many dangers with this, which can mean the senior managers may suffer from hubris (i.e. a belief in their own infallibility), or to make wrong decisions or fail to see future dangers. This is particularly prominent in sport, given its focus as a people business. Consequently it is increasingly important to have two-way flows of communication, which Torkildsen (2005, p. 407) argues is both practical and moral. While the practical aspects may be relatively clear, such as checking on understanding, or creating a sense of involvement in the organisation, the moral considerations are a little more challenging to articulate. They can relate to issues where poor practice may be taking place, which may relate to safety, or behaviour which is morally wrong. It begins to enter into the area of whistleblowing, which has seen some important cases in the area of sport, which can range from issues of drug-taking, to bribery. Whistleblowing has become an important form of communication to improve practice with many countries offering legal protection to those willing to expose poor management practices. Examples of whistleblowing even extend to major events like the London Olympics in 2012 where a hotline was set up as part of a wider risk-management strategy. Confidential whistleblowing hotlines are now seen as best practice.

HUMAN SKILLS: LEADERSHIP

When we are teaching, we will often ask our students to list the qualities of good management and the skills of good leadership. What is always striking is how much the two lists can overlap. These two concepts, whilst intimately related, do however have distinct attributes. To illustrate this overlap, we can use Goleman's comprehensive study of over 3,000 middle-level managers, in which he identified a number of leadership styles which are also sometimes referred to as management styles in various management databases. When you look at Goleman's (2000) six styles it can be easier to see why the terms can become mixed up. The styles are:

- pacesetting leader
- authoritarian leader
- affiliate leader
- coaching leader
- coercive leader
- democratic leader.

As with everything in this book there will be other variations, but we only need to focus on the basics here; those that range from democratic to authoritarian styles. Although some writers such as Adair and Reed (2003, p. 45) are critical of the use of these terms, it should also be appreciated that the styles used should, in theory, vary according to the context, the staff and what needs to be achieved. Wolsey (2011, p. 342) notes that one of the ways that management and leadership is sometimes distinguished is that management functions can be taught, whereas leadership skills are learnt from doing. In practice, this distinction is far more blurred. Some writers on management, such as Adair (1990), advocate the use of training and skills in leadership, which he believes can be learnt, whereby the old adage that 'leaders are born, not made' is one which is too simplistic, denying how people can learn and grow into leadership roles.

Looking at the functions and roles of management, it is clear that someone performing these roles will help maintain the organisation. When a manager also combines good management with good leadership, this creates the potential to transform the organisation. Inspiration, for example, can be more effective than simple management practice to shape and change organisations for the better. Whilst a good leader may also be an effective in some areas of management, what is often expected is that something more is done; of course the corollary of this is that a manager who fails as a leader can harm the organisation.

There is little doubt about the importance we now attach to leadership. In terms of organisational theory and management, along with the study of motivational theory, it perhaps forms the second key pillar for the subject area of organisational and management theory. In Table 3.4 a summary of the key leadership theories are given to give a sense of how thinking has changed over time, such as how the initial study of leadership simply focused on the traits of prominent political leaders. Whilst personal characteristics can still play a part, they are now considered as one element which governs the effectiveness of leadership. In essence, leadership effectiveness will be shaped by the leadership style or behaviour that they adopt (e.g. democratic or authoritarian), the context and the situation that they find themselves in (contingency theories), such as if the group is experienced or inexperienced, or if it is a crisis situation, needing swift, decisive decisions. How well they communicate and can represent their ideas, decisions or visions will influence the degree that they are transformational leaders.

Whether leaders are in a management role, or are playing their part in a team, can have a vital role in establishing, developing and embodying organisational culture or operational ethos. Organisational culture is another important area for business effectiveness. Over the years, in many countries, there have been examples of organisational operating cultures which could be characterised by institutional racism, sexism, bullying or corruption. Here you must have good leadership skills to change culture. This has certainly been true in sport. Reflect back to Chapter 2 where we talked about the people who embody the sport organisation and who are expected to give it leadership, but have, at times, been found wanting in their ethical leadership and values.

Table 3.4   Examples of key leadership theories and writers

Category	Examples of writers and theories
Trait theories	Early theories looked at how factors such as personality, self-confidence, intelligence and physical characteristics influenced leadership. They were very inconsistent and limited.
Behaviourist/ personality theories	Alternative factors were looked at, such as how the behaviour of the person influenced the leadership effectiveness. Blake and Mouton (1981) placed managers on a grid, depending on how concerned, or how much they prioritise people or the needs of the business or production. Five key categories were identified, which were: country-club manager, team manager, organisational, impoverished management or authority and obedience. Tannenbaum and Schmidt (1958) developed a continuum model, related to the freedom that the manager gives to staff. A manager can adopt a number of leadership approaches, which related to: A tells, B sells, C and D consults, E shares, F and G delegates. As one goes from tells, to delegates, the staff steadily gain more freedom.
Contingency / situational leadership	Other leadership theories have developed which consider how the context can influence the effectiveness of certain leadership styles. There are a number of theories such as: Wosley (2011, p. 344) gives a useful insight in relation to how styles can be adapted depending on the nature of the group, so that a very experienced team of people, may respond to a less directive approach. They present their work in a four part grid, with the key categories described as: supporting (high supportive, low directive); coaching (high directive, high supportive); delegating (low supporting and low directive); directing (high directing and low supportive).
Transformational leaders	The idea of transformational leadership refers to how management practice can shift the ethos or working practices of an organisation. An example of a transformational theory relates to Weese (1996) who developed the five C's model of Leadership and the idea of visionary leadership, with each C relating to: C1 credible character (leaders have respect and perceived as trustworthy); C2 compelling vision (followers believe in the leader and in the vision); C3 charismatic communicator (good communication skills heighten leaders' standing); C4 contagious enthusiasm (leader excites and inspired others to go beyond the call of duty); C5 culture builder (beliefs, values and attitudes shape and interpret behaviour of a group).

TEAM DEVELOPMENT

Hoye *et al.* (2012 p. 126) used President Roosevelt's quote to illustrate not only the importance of teams, but also about delegation and leadership. He says:

> The best executive is the one who has sense enough to pick good men to do what he wants done, and self-restraint enough to keep from meddling with them while they do it.
>
> (Hoye *et al.* 2012, p. 146 citing Roosevelt)

We've already looked at the aspects of team work relating to delegation, motivation and leadership. However, as a manager you need to understand the importance of a team and how it functions. When you undertake group work as part of your studies you will experience tension and difficulty which can destabilise a project. In the case of an organisation this can be challenging with relationships breaking down and the effective achievement of objectives becoming impossible. The critical question here will be how a manager can get the team to perform and work together effectively. Elements of good delegation will be important here, along with how to motivate and ensuring everyone is doing their task. Goal-setting will help here as will positive reinforcement. Most of all you will need to have developed good relationships with your team.

Leadership and team development can be intimately related. We regularly hear stories in sport about the importance of leadership, such as how a team captain can unite a team and motivate others to succeed. At other times, for more mature teams, one can sometimes hear expressions that all the team members were 'leaders on the pitch'. Additionally, there can be instances of how other factors, such as a crisis, can forge a tight team identity or an *ésprit de corps*, which means the team members can work together more effectively. Whilst there may be an expectation for a manager to exhibit good leadership qualities, leadership should also be shown within teams. Leadership, in short, should not be bound by the organisational hierarchy.

TRANSFERRING SKILLS

We explained in Chapter 1 how sport has often been presented with having many virtues, which have the potential to benefit the individual, an organisation or society. We also noted that at times these benefits can often be overstated, or have little evidence to support the claims. In terms of how sport can help organisations and businesses, there are four broad areas which can be considered:

- creating opportunities for sport and active recreation can help motivate staff and look after their sense of wellbeing;
- skills learnt by an individual playing sport can be transferred to other working environments;
- skills learnt about organising sport and teams can be transferred to help structure organisations;
- skills learnt in working environments can be transferred back to organise sport.

The playing of sport and active recreation was discussed in Chapter 2 which allows us to examine the last three items here. From an individual point of view, it can be argued that sport can be a way for personal development. Indeed, as Chapter 2 illustrated, that was a founding belief for many of the public schools in Britain which helped drive the expansion of sports. Skills such as discipline, hard work, a winning mentality, discipline of the mind and body, being gracious in defeat, modest in victory, individualism replaced by team work and being goal-driven can often be extolled as part of the virtues of sport. It is one of the reasons why sport is presented as a means to deal with various social problems, such as those relating to crime and social disorder.

But these are very sweeping generalisations. To establish whether they are transferrable takes some critical appraisal. For example, some of the claimed benefits of sport may only work for some team games. In others it may encourage selfish individualism. Similarly, the ideas of the work ethic and winning may actually only apply to a very small group of athletes, who are professional or semi-professional; for most people's experience of playing sport there will be no transfer of benefit. Indeed, it can be quite remarkable how little students who study and play sport can actually transfer the elements of teamwork and discipline to assignment work. Some do, some do not. It is, to say the least, a very ambiguous relationship. Yes it is possible to find examples of elite athletes who have gone on to be very successful in business, but then it can also be possible to find numerous others who have failed. Often the crucial ingredient is the capacity to reflect on what has taken place and having the ability to transfer the context of the experience to different situations.

Of perhaps more importance is how theories and practices used in sport can be transferred to business. One of the interesting developments in management and leadership theory has been the development of the idea that staff should be coached and mentored. Peters (1996, cited in Liu *et al.* 1998) has been a keen advocate of this approach, which in essence is about managers developing a more supportive and intimate relationship with staff, which is about encouragement, goal setting and supporting. Increasingly, the term coaching is being used in management. What this refers to is the idea of guiding people through activities, training them to perform better and clearly communicating what needs to be done. It moves towards the area of 'enabling' people to do more and improving performance; just as a coach can improve skill development, physical fitness and mental discipline, so to, the theory goes, can these principles be adapted to a business organisation context.

In other areas, sport, certainly at the elite level, provides many attractive metaphors for business, with the themes of winning, teamwork, developing an *ésprit de corps* and passion all being attractive qualities to try and harness and transfer. Finally, as Box 3.1 illustrates, it is also interesting to observe how some of the more successful sport coaches and managers around the world in recent times have also been keen to learn from business, even the military, in shaping their coaching approaches.

BOX 3.1   HOW TO ORGANISE A WINNING TEAM AND WHAT CAN BE LEARNT FOR BUSINESS?

When Clive Woodward won the Rugby World Cup with England in 2003, his approach and style of management was of interest not only for other rugby nations, but to others in sport and, interestingly, to businesses in general. Woodward, in a variety of interviews and articles, has identified a number of key factors which explain his team's success, which anyone can learn from, such these adapted points from Campbell (2004) and Woodward (2005):

- *Attention to detail:* every aspect of players' training and preparation is scrutinised. This is now common in all levels of elite sport, with David Brailsford, who helped deliver incredible sport success for UK cycling, refining this into the notion of incremental marginal gains (i.e. the difference between winning and losing at the elite level can be so fine, anything which can give a slight advantage should be considered).
- *Preparation and planning:* you need to know about your opposition, organise specialist advice and test yourselves, so that you can compete without fear.
- *Ruthless decision making:* in order to win, there can be no room for sentiment or for people who do not pull their weight.
- *Loyalty and treat players as adults:* this related to the trust put in the team members and seeing them as all leaders, where they all needed to have the same tactical awareness of the game, not simply rely on one individual. Also, there was an expectation that the athlete and the team would stick together, removing anyone who was critical, so as to create a positive environment.
- *Unreasonable ambition and belief:* despite some difficult early games and criticisms, he remained clear and fixed on his overall ambition, which all the team members were committed to.
- *Flexibility:* although highly organised, there had to be capacity for the team to be able to adapt as circumstances changed.

There are many variations to the list, but it should be clear how some of the ideas would be attractive to some business managers.

One of the areas, ruthless decision making, could be attractive to some managers, particularly those in a competitive commercial environment, whilst for others this may not be such a critical principle, particularly if their work relates to social objectives. What was also interesting was how Woodward changed the operating culture of the team, whereby he brought in many of the principles of management theory, such as goal setting, to help structure the whole approach to the team preparation. Interestingly, it was an approach which did not work as well for the tour which he led to New Zealand as part of the 2005 Lions tour.

CONCLUSION

Intuitively, we know what managers do. They deal with problems; they need to make decisions; they give orders and instruction; they coordinate; they hire and fire; and they design programmes. The list can go on, so to help it is useful to 'tidy' what can be a long list into some convenient categories. To begin with, Fayol's management functions list, although written over a hundred years ago, still gives a useful summary of some of the key functions which a manager must do. It is however more of a description, and so less helpful in trying to identify what good managers must do. Here, the elaboration of roles and skills are useful, as they give a set of concepts which you can reflect upon and consider your own strengths and weaknesses in these areas. It should also be appreciated that management is considered more art than science and that humanistic theories are becoming more important.

When looking at the many theories and tools it may seem over-whelming and questions raised as to how they can all be applied. The point is that they don't need to. A critical part of the theories is that they give concepts with which to reflect and analyse problems. As theories and concepts are explored in more depth (as they will need to be) they can continue to help in the analysis of the problems.

In terms of sport organisations which need management, there is immense variation in their purpose (e.g. profit or social objectives), their scale (e.g. from a few people volunteering to thousands of people in paid employment) and the need for formal structures and management (e.g. egalitarian structures with no one person in charge, to a clear organised hierarchy of management). When managing these structures, there is no reason why the more generic management theories cannot be applied to their management. It is some of the more technical expertise where more specific knowledge and sensitivity about sport is needed.

One of the interesting developments is how values and skills learnt in sport can be transferred to working environments and, just as importantly, how management skills learnt in business can be transferred to the management of sport. In terms of the first point, the evidence is still mixed, but sport provides many powerful, emotive analogies to the world of business. In terms of sport learning from business, this has been long overdue, where there are numerous examples of sport organisations which have been mismanaged, whereby former athletes who were commanding in their sport, fail to be effective leaders of an organisation.

4

THE BUSINESS FUNCTIONS OF SPORT MANAGEMENT

INTRODUCTION

Having been through the emergence of sport management as a functional discipline and having considered the foundations upon which the industry has been built, it's important to start thinking about what managers actually do in sport. Consequently, we've designed this chapter to examine some of the classic, core business subject areas or as they will be called here, business functions, that you will likely need to study and be involved with. Essentially, these functions are based around the areas of marketing, finance and human resource (HR) management. Of course, in practice these extend into many other more discrete disciplines such as economics, project management and even research methods but these are outside the scope of a 'Basics' text.

We will review these core business functions in relation to the management functions discussed in Chapter 3. Next, we will define the three key business functions and explain their importance in relation to sport management. In addition a brief identification of the key concepts which need to be understood are examined in relation to each area. One important point to appreciate here is that although the three areas are explained, a practising sport manager will often have to operate in all of the business functional areas. This means that you need a toolbox of skills that you can apply to work and make sure that each function works together with the others. Crudely speaking, if you identify some human resource requirements but don't manage the money, you can't meet your objectives.

MANAGEMENT FUNCTIONS AND BUSINESS FUNCTIONS

As we have touched on elsewhere, sport businesses and organisations exist to either achieve a profit, achieve some broader social objectives, or to encourage people to participate in some form of sport and physical activity to promote the benefits of healthy living. A little simplistic perhaps, but it helps distil what makes an organisation viable and so continue to operate. Of course, when you look at a range of sport organisations from different economic sectors (discussed in Chapter 6), you can often see many areas of overlap, such as commercial organisations which exist primarily for profit, but which may also have many social objectives, or sport organisations which have a focus on social objectives, may behave more like a commercial organisation in order to generate additional revenue. Yet whilst there will be overlaps, the simple essence relating to profit, social objectives or simple membership, helps give a convenient shorthand to describe the essential purpose of the organisation.

In order for a business to be successful and viable managers must employ the key *management functions* effectively (i.e. the planning, control, coordination, communication and organistion we discussed in Chapter 3), towards the management of three essential *business functional areas*, which are based around the management of:

- *Customers/stakeholders:* these relate to the marketing function, which asks a variety of questions such as: what is the point of its service or product? Who is it for? What does it give them?

- *People/staffing:* these relate to the HR function, which asks such questions as: how are people employed and used to make the product or produce the service? Are they paid or volunteers? Are legal regulations complied with?
- *Money/finances:* these relate to the finance functions, which ask questions such as: How is money managed? Is there adequate income coming in? Are costs and expenditure properly controlled? Are there robust financial controls?

It is worthwhile emphasising the difference between management functions and business functions. If you look at Figure 4.1, you will notice that all the management functions can be applied to the different business functions. In addition, both these business and management functions can be utilised at all the different levels of management, as will be discussed in Chapter 5.

When looking at the many roles available in sport management, it is possible to find specialist appointments in each of these functional business areas, where there may

BUSINESS FUNCTIONS	MANAGEMENT FUNCTIONS	Plan	Control	Communicate	Monitor	Lead	Relevant at all levels of management (strategic, project and operational)
People / marketing							
Money / finance							
Staffing / HR							
Other / miscellaneous							
Relevant at all levels of management (strategic, project and operational)							

Figure 4.1 The relationship of business and management functions and the levels of management

also be additional requirement to have a relevant professional qualification, certainly in some of the very large sport organisations. These additional qualifications are normally studied for 'on the job' or as continuing professional development (CPD) and can range from memberships with the Chartered Institute of Management Accountants (or the Association of Chartered Certified Accountants) if you wish to work directly in the function of financial management, the Chartered Institute of Marketing if you wish to be a professional marketer, or the Chartered Institute of Personnel and Development if, you guessed it, you want to work directly in the management and development of people (HR).

In Table 4.1 a range of jobs are given to illustrate how employment opportunities can relate to specific business functions, in different sectors and focus on different levels of management.

Another observation, which we will return to in Chapter 8, relates to how future managers will need to be more flexible and adaptable. Across the business world, more and more jobs are being developed whereby they may focus on a particular business function, but will also require an understanding of the other business functional areas, as a number of the examples in Table 4.1 illustrate, such as the marketing job for hockey (job 1) also requiring an understanding of finance. Indeed, as the business of sport develops, there are many new specialist types of jobs being created, such as those relating to event management, but which still require an understanding of staffing, customers and money, but which are applied to more specialist types of work.

FUNCTIONAL BUSINESS DISCIPLINES: MARKETING

It is not unusual in business- and marketing-related literature to see a claim made that marketing should be a central function of all business management. Watt (1998), for example, states quite bluntly that businesses have only two functions: marketing and innovation. This may come as a surprise to some if you simply associate marketing with

Table 4.1 Examples of different jobs based in the key business functions

Job 1 – Specific marketing function for a governing body of sport (voluntary sector)

A job advertised by England Hockey (governing body for English hockey) related to sales and marketing. The role had a specialist function in terms of marketing campaigns (advertising function) to increase participation, particularly in terms of hospitality and major events, retail and casual hockey participation. A key part of the role was to strengthen the hockey brand and to meet and exceed revenue and net profit targets. The job does not involve the writing of strategy, rather its implementation and so the job is more operational and project based in the level of management. The need to forecast monthly and annual revenue streams does show how it overlaps with areas of finance which can feed into strategic processes. In terms of experience, relevant marketing qualifications (e.g the Chartered Institute of Marketing) were required, along with proven experience of managing budgets and both leading a team, or being a good team player and being innovative, with good communication skills, organisational and time management skills, creativity and the 'ability to think laterally'.

Job 2 – Human resource manager for a sport manufacturer (private sector)

A job advertised by the Adidas sport manufacturer based in America focused on human resource elements. The job entailed human relations management to support the areas of employee engagement, employee relations, performance/ talent management, recruitment, immigration and compensation. There was a strong operational focus to implement HR initiatives, programs and policies. Also, what was of interest was how the role stated that the manager needed to be an 'ear and a coach', to help staff 'navigate job issues, career development etc.' The role was very much of the specialist type function, where the work would involve focusing on aspects of recruitment, compensation and training. In terms of skills, these related to HRIS and SAP experience, communicate effectively, be a strong team player and have the ability to work with diverse groups, along with being educated to degree level with emphasis in human resource management or psychology preferred.

Job 3 – Regional account manager (specialised private sector)

A job advertised for Harlands Group in the UK is an example of an indirect sport-related organisation, whereby its business relates to providing systems which manage the direct debits and membership management systems for fitness centres. Despite the title, there was in fact a strong marketing function related to the job, as it involved increasing sales, contact existing clients and further developing the client base. Interestingly, one of the attributes needed for the job was bringing an existing network of contacts, along with operational and sales experience in the health club market.

Job 4 – Qualified accountant (private, small enterprise)

A job advertised by a SME sports retailer related to someone who was a qualified accountant to add value in an 'all round' finance manager role. The role involved preparing monthly management accounts, reviewing end-of-year accounts, presenting results to senior stakeholders, financial planning and analysis, with particular focus on margin, cost and profit across the balance sheet. They needed to be CIMA/ACCA qualified with experience in retail.

advertising or selling. Whilst these are parts of marketing, they do not represent the essence of marketing. When you look at how marketing is defined, the claims for its centrality in all businesses' management become clear, for which the sport sector is no exception.

The Chartered Institute of Marketing (CIM) definition states that marketing was 'the management process responsible for identifying, anticipating and satisfying customer requirements profitably' (CIM 2009). This is a perfect message when trying to understand what marketing is actually about and demonstrates how important the function is to the lifecycle of the business. The elements relating to 'identifying, anticipating and satisfying customer requirements' are crucial, whereby businesses need to understand just what it is that customers want from their goods and services. It helps to define what customers really need from the business which means that the business can develop products and services to meet these needs. Once you have identified the product or service you can work out how best to deliver that to the customer (to satisfy them). For commercial organisations, if they get this wrong then there is no profit; and if there is no profit, then they will struggle to continue being a viable business enterprise. The latter part of the message 'profitable' is a vital addition here.

By contrast, and remember we are trying to get you to think a little more broadly here, there are two key problems with the CIM marketing definition. The first relates to the narrow focus on *wants*. At times it may be better to focus on *needs* and we give a full discussion as to why this is the case in Chapter 7. The second problem relates to the focus on 'profit', which, as it has been stated many times, is not the key organisational purpose of all sport organisations. The inference one could take from this is that non-profit sport organisations do not need to use marketing theories, concepts and practices – but this is a ludicrous proposition. It is just as important for non-profit sport organisations to understand their customers', clients' and key stakeholders' needs and wants, with services designed to meet these needs. The only difference is that it is not necessarily done for profit, hence the growth in what is sometimes called social marketing.

Contemporary marketing practices have developed to reflect some of these demands to market for not-for-profit rationales. Initially, when marketing was becoming a more coherent and a distinct business function in 1950s corporate America, there was clearly an emphasis on finding ways to sell products for a profit. Since those times, the world has changed in profound ways, particularly in relation to how businesses need to think about issues relating to corporate social responsibility (CSR), which can relate to the environment, human rights, animal welfare and so on (this is again outside the scope of this introduction to sport management text). This issue though is a good example of how the core business functions begin to blur. People working in finance will sometimes talk about a triple bottom line. A rather broad term but one that essentially means they must consider profit, people and planet (we'll come back to the profit part later). Into this has been the growth of how governments, agencies and not-for-profit organisations can use marketing theory and processes to help them achieve their social objectives more effectively and efficiently. This is why marketing definitions have evolved. Influential scholars in the subject of marketing such as Kotler, have developed more expansive definitions to articulate what marketing is:

> Marketing is a social and managerial process by which individuals and groups obtain what they need and want through creating and exchanging products and value with others
>
> (Kotler 1988) p. 3)

You can see the differences between Kotler's point and the earlier definition from the Chartered Institute of Marketing. The dates here are less important; the change in some of the narrative perhaps more so. But, before we get knee-deep in these definitions and academic arguments let's pause for thought. For you, at entry level at least, we need to focus on the following key points when looking at marketing and sport management:

- Marketing can be understood as a business philosophy where managers should focus on putting the needs of the customers or other key stakeholders first. This should be central to their management approach.
- Marketing should be understood as a practical management process, which utilises many essential concepts, theories and management tools to try and design goods and services to meet the needs and wants of the key stakeholders, for profit or to achieve social objectives.
- Sport managers need to appreciate the differences between how sport products (the tangible goods that people can buy) and sport services can be marketed, as sport services are distinguished from products by being: perishable (i.e. once a time slot for a service has gone, it can never be resold); intangibility (i.e. a service which you may purchase cannot be scrutinised or tried in the same way, as say for example an article of clothing); inseparability (the service must be consumed at the time of purchase); and variability (as humans can be unpredictable in their behaviour which can mean there is more potential for variability in services).

A FEW KEY CONCEPTS RELATING TO MARKETING

It stands to reason that if there is a professional body that supports the marketing industry that there will be many concepts and ideas that you could examine. Indeed there are reams of books that cover the topic of marketing. This means we can't cover everything here; this book is meant to cover the basics after all. Instead what we have chosen to do here is run through a few key concepts that our own students have told us that they have needed to use in the sport industry when they have graduated and started to work, which are:

- *Different market orientations:* in marketing there are some very useful terms which can describe the type of marketing focus or orientation it has. The type of orientations can be placed in a broad historical framework, which are: the production concept which suggests that consumers favour goods that are widely available and cheap; the *product concept* where consumers favour those products that offer quality and performance, with the belief that people love the product whatever happens. This can be adapted for public leisure facilities where it is possible to talk about being 'facility-orientated' (Torkildsen 2005, p. 134) whereby managers focus on the facility rather than what it can give to customers; the *selling concept* which uses aggressive selling and promotion techniques to encourage purchases, or 'coaxing' people to buy the products; the *marketing concept* which is key to achieving organisation goals and is about determining the needs and wants of target groups and then satisfying these needs; the *social market concept* and the notion of satisfying needs in a way that preserves or enhances the consumer and society's well-being, which can be extended to the natural environment and educational campaigns, such as those relating to health, or dealing with issues of racism in sport.

- *Marketing mix and the 4 Ps:* even if you are new to the field of management or marketing in general, you have probably heard of the marketing mix. The classic works examined how managers need to control the 4 Ps (the marketing mix), which are: product (understanding what the customer wants from the product, how they use it etc.); price (What is the price customers are willing to pay? How does it compare with competitors? etc.); place (Where can customers get the product from? Considering the importance of location etc.); promotion (How will you communicate or tell key target groups about the service and product? What methods are used, such how to use posters, leaflets, word of mouth, news stories, social media). Over recent years, there have been a number of adaptions to the 4Ps, such as adding people (How you work and use the people who deal with your service?) and the process (How is the service delivered? How are people managed in queues?), or even using the 4 Cs (consumer, cost, communication and convenience).

- *Business environment:* a critical part of the marketing function is to understand how the external business environment creates market opportunities or threats. Aspects of this have already been discussed in Chapter 2 where we illustrated how changes, categorised around the PEST categories, constantly drive opportunistic or threatening change (see also Chapter 5 and the discussion on strategy).

- *Product and industry lifecycle:* this concept is invaluable, as it acts as a reminder that unless the sport manager innovates and adapts to change, then their product or service can move through a process of *growth, maturity* and then *decline.* The challenge is to not necessarily simply stop the decline, but to consider how they can rejuvenate the service or product, as Box 4.1 illustrates in relation to football. Sometimes the term industry lifecycle may be seen, essentially referring to a how an entire industry sector can go through this pattern of growth, maturity and decline, as shown in Box 4.1.

- *Target markets and segmentation:* sport products and services will have many different types of users, who may consume at different times and in many different ways. In marketing, this dividing up of the population into particular groups is called segmentation. Sometimes in sport, the term target market may be used, but it essentially refers to the same thing. How a population can be segmented will vary, depending on how effectively it meets their needs and wants, as will be explained in Chapter 7.

FINANCIAL FUNCTION

Anyone working in business, let alone those working in sport, cannot afford to ignore the functions of finance and the impact that good or bad financial decisions can have on their organisation. To put it simply and boldly, all management decisions will have financial implications. As sport and leisure managers you need to understand the financial side of the industry so that you can provide good, cost-effective solutions to an array of complex problems and an increasingly changeable market. We've drawn a number of lines already when it comes to business objectives but can reaffirm them here. A sport business will exist either to make a profit or to meet social

BOX 4.1   THE MARKETING OF ENGLISH FOOTBALL

Football or soccer gives an interesting example to illustrate a variety of sport management and marketing concepts.

Figure 4.2 shows English football attendance from 1947 and it gives an illustration of the product life cycle. Looking at the graph, it shows that up until 1950s, football was still in a *growth* stage, when it begins to *mature* then go into a steady and consistent *decline*, with a few spikes which temporarily slow the decline (such as England winning the world cup in 1966). From the 1990s the pattern is of *rejuvenation*, as football in England goes through some radical transformations, being *rebranded* and *positioned*, but which seems to have gone through the growth stage and is nearing maturity, which, unless there are more changes, may mean that another period of decline may well begin. Whilst the market for growing football in England may be at saturation point, this is not the same for the overseas market, hence how different premiership clubs, such as Manchester United or Liverpool, attempt to grow a fan base in many Asian countries, such as in China or India, as this offers different funding streams and different markets to enjoy the service.

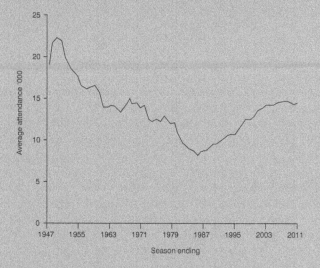

Figure 4.2   English Football League overall attendances by season (source: Critcher 1982, RowZ 2014)

The factors which drove the steady decline were varied, many of which related to the *external business environment*, such as social changes, new leisure activities competing for time, various economic structural changes and even poor performances of the international team. The length of the decline can also be put down to poor management with many clubs and the governing body being *product orientated*: a belief that people were simply interested in football, failing to understand what it gives, such as entertainment or an opportunity for social interaction. During the period of decline, the brand image of football became a negative one, associated with hooliganism, violence and one that could quite literally cost you your life, as the 1987 Bradford stadium fire, or the 1989 Hillsborough disaster demonstrated. Football, in England, was in trouble. Yet it was changes in the external business environment which also created opportunities, particularly in relation to the growth in satellite communications and the huge amounts of money that began to pour into the game. The result was that football could reposition itself, where the top clubs could target high-quality corporate hospitality niches, but changes which have generated many criticisms and lively discussions.

objectives (this was all covered in Chapter 1). Whilst this might lead you to believe that for the latter organisations, financial management is less important, this would be a profoundly misplaced and irresponsible judgement. Whilst the managers may not need to make a profit, they will still have a duty to maximise the effectiveness and impacts of the money they do spend in their attempts of using sport to deliver on social objectives. Indeed, because this money comes from charitable donations or peoples' taxes (i.e the money that local or central government may give to subsidise or support activities), one can even argue that managers have a moral responsibility to use money in both an efficient and effective manner.

We can acknowledge that some sport organisations are not financially motivated but need to stress the importance of financial management and responsibility as mandatory requirements that we should place on all organisations. Before you start to worry though, it's worth getting something straight. Finance is not simply about numbers and you do not have to be a skilled mathematician to understand financial information (it's also much less subjective than the other two functional areas covered in this chapter).

DEFINING FINANCIAL MANAGEMENT

Before we get too far into the discussion about what financial management is and the types of information you will need to use, let's just take a step back and work out why the management of finance is so important. The professionalisation of sport has led to many opportunities, such as: investment in and growth of professional team sports (the Glazer takeover of Manchester United in 2005, for example); the huge sums of money paid by broadcasters to show major events (world title boxing competitions routinely deliver multi-million dollar purses); sponsorship requirements (just think how many brands are splashed on F1 cars and driver suits); or the growth of private-sector health and fitness centres around the world.

Some writers, such as Wilson (2011) and Stewart (2014), illustrate how sport and leisure has established a mechanism for creating personal meaning and identity, of which the purchasing of an expensive replica team shirts is a key tangible expression of this cultural identity. The Premier League in the UK in 2015 signed a £5.136bn deal to sell TV rights, many sportsmen and women earn multi-million dollar salaries and gambling on sport is the fastest growing sector of the market. The point is that it shows how managers must both seek and manage many streams of revenue, whereby even for non-profit organisations, looking for additional ways to bring in new revenue streams of income can be just as important.

Despite all of this, sport has often lagged behind other business sectors in terms of financial management. For the most part sport marketing, planning, HR and strategy have dominated sport management education programmes with financial management being overlooked. It remains though one of the most influential functions that you can master and forms a critical underpinning for all marketing and HR decisions. At the most fundamental level though, as Wilson (2011) indicates, every organisation, ranging from multi-million pound operations through to small, local, voluntary sport clubs, needs to produce a set of financial statements every year. This means that communicating and managing this information is one of those skills required in your management toolbox.

For the purposes of this section though, we need to focus on some of the basics, namely: the difference between financial and management accounting; financial statements; and the budgetary process. The function of finance, at the 'Basics' level at least, is much more about 'tools' than concepts.

THE DIFFERENCE BETWEEN FINANCIAL AND MANAGEMENT ACCOUNTS

You'd be forgiven for thinking that accounts were only available in one format, that there was a standard way of presenting such information. However, nothing in management is that straightforward and in finance there are two types of accounts: financial and management. In reality the development of any accounting information would be undertaken by an accountant who had qualified with the relevant professional body (we referred to the Chartered Institute of Management Accountants and the Association of Chartered Certified Accountants earlier in this chapter). The differences between the two accounts are:

- Financial accounts are historical, they look back at what has been. They also tend to be used by external groups, normally those making investment decisions, whether that is lending money, providing a future payment facility for stocks and so on.
- Management accounting by contrast is concerned with the examination of financial information that looks to the future. It's much better to use management accounting information for planning, decision making and control purposes as you are working with more up-to-date data.

Unlike financial accounts, management accounts are not a statutory requirement and as such tend to be only used by internal members of staff, rarely being made available for more public scrutiny. They are private and can be rather sensitive, particularly when they look at pricing, long-term decisions and budgeting.

In larger sport organisations financial and management accounts should work hand-in-hand. Even though the law stipulates that financial accounts should be constructed, the reality is that any manager will need to control costs appropriately and ensure that they can pay their debts as they fall due. It also stands to reason that for commercial orientated businesses, the selling price should be higher than the cost, thus allowing the organisation to make a surplus (or profit). Proper planning, decision-making and control management here will allow the organisation to more adequately meet its objectives. To that end we believe that the modern sport manager needs to have a firm grasp of the core principles of management accounting given its alignment with management functions of planning, decision-making and control and specifically: budgeting, break-even analysis (ensuring costs are covered in pricing decisions) and costing projects, products and services.

All of this talk of planning, decision-making and control does not necessarily need to focus on profit, more, the effective use of resources. Remember, profit is not the only basis of success and don't confuse profit with revenue (students often use the terms inter-changeably, but this should be avoided). This is also why good financial management is needed at all levels of the management pyramid (project, operation, strategic discussed in Chapter 5). It is vital that sport managers appreciate that sport services will often operate at a loss. This may be necessary to achieve social objectives and may well be supported by local or central government subsidy. This is perfectly acceptable, but cannot be abused. Proper financial controls are important so that all projects provide value for money and are sustainable.

The final point we need to make in this section is that borrowing is not necessarily a bad thing. There are plenty of high-profile financial failures in sport, such as: the losses incurred when staging major sport competitions such as the Olympics; the winding-up of professional sport entities; or the bankruptcy of sport stars or local organisations. Most will point at loans (or borrowing) as the problem. Rest assured though, the borrowing isn't the problem, it's the lack of adequate financial planning to ensure that debts can be paid when they fall due and that interest payments can be serviced by the revenues generated. Over-ambition and lack of planning cause the problem!

FINANCIAL STATEMENTS

As we mentioned earlier, all organisations need to produce financial statements by law and it tends not to matter where you are based in the world: all organisations must produce them. The detail contained within these statements will vary according to the size of the business however; so many sport organisations will only need summarised statements or basic outlines for the purposes of their annual general meetings. Traditionally, when we talk about financial statements, we are referring to three main items, which are: the balance sheet; the income statement (or profit and loss account); and the cash flow statement. Some not-for-profit organisations may use slightly different terminology, but the basic principles remain the same.

Being able to read the information contained within the three main financial statements is important. The following outlines the key elements which each statement must consider:

- *The balance sheet* provides a list of all of the things a business owns and uses. These are called assets. It also details the things that the business owes (liabilities) and the overall value of the business (capital/equity). The balance sheet provides us with a statement of an organisation's financial position. That is to say we can work out what the business owns and what it owes so that we can work out how its long-term prospects look.
- *The income statement* by contrast helps us to examine an organisation's financial performance by matching income

earned (revenue) with all the things the organisation spent money on (expenditure). This helps us to work out whether the business has made an annual profit or loss and most importantly where the highest levels of expenditure are. By comparing the accounts from two consecutive years we can also establish if the business has grown i.e. performed better between years.

- *The cash flow statement* is an often overlooked item. This provides you with one of the simplest ways to monitor financial performance by providing information about when money comes in and when money leaves an organisation. Effective management of the inflows and outflows is vital for planning and good cash flow management can often be the difference between success and failure. The monitoring of the monthly cash position of an organisation is achieved via the budgetary process (examined in a moment) and then summarised in a cash flow statement at the end of the financial year. We refer to movements in cash here and not any movements in profit. You cannot live on profit, as it is not tangible, that is to say, you never have profit in your hand and you can't spend it. It's a number on a financial statement rather than something you can genuinely use. Cash is king and is the only resource you can use to manage your way out of trouble or capitalise on growth (at least in smaller sport organisations).

THE BUDGETARY PROCESS

Management accounting will involve you being much more proactive in a management role, as the information generated is used for a number of things from budgeting, to pricing decisions for products and services (see Box 4.2 for an example of management accounting information in practice). The information will also need to be presented in such a way that it is clear and understandable for a specific audience. This is different to financial accounting which is provided to a variety of external stakeholders. The real benefit of management accounting information though is the fact that it is concerned with the efficient and effective use of resources. To that end, while budgeting is one of a variety of management accounting tools that you will need in a managerial position, it is probably the most important one you will use. Particularly at entry level and while continuing to learn.

Budgeting is principally concerned with the estimation of revenues, costs, and expenses incurred when implementing plans. Understanding and being able to apply conventional budgeting techniques can often be the first step in managing finance effectively in any organisation and, when done properly, can lead to large gains. When manifested these 'gains' can be in terms of cost savings, more appropriate pricing, better negotiation of credit facilities, more effective use of payroll arrangements and even bonus schemes for employees or discounts for customers. All of the above will hinge on the effective management of resources.

Ostensibly, a budget is a plan of action expressed in financial terms. They can often be presented in a summary form or produced for discrete projects, products or services so that profit can be measured on a case-by-case basis. Ideally a budget should cover all of the activities involved in an organisation and should involve as many staff as possible in the planning process. This will help ensure that plans are communicated effectively. Ultimately a budget must be realistic and ensure that it is directly related to the organisation's objectives.

While larger organisations will spend a great deal of time over their budgeting process, moving through lots of iterations and consultations, smaller organisations may simply provide a list of expected income and expenditure for a project, planned activity or day-to-day operations. If expenditure exceeds income for profit orientated businesses, the budget will naturally need to be re-examined and consideration given to cheaper alternatives. This is where negotiations with other departments will be important.

It is important that budgeting plays a central role in keeping an organisation's finances on track and should ensure that debts are paid as they fall due. Proper adherence to budgets will also ensure that there are no nasty surprises when the financial accountant draws up the year-end financial statements. Good budgeting will normally be based on the following information:

- the financial history of the organisation;
- the general economic climate;
- income and expenditure that is reasonably expected to be generated with the resources available (this is vital and is so often over-estimated); and
- data from competitors.

In advance of the trading year, good managers will spend time developing their budgets and will ensure the most recent data is used. It forces you to think ahead, consider bumps in the road and make a decent plan of action. For sport organisations we often suggest the use of zero-based budgets. These budgets essentially start with a blank sheet of paper and ask questions based on the need for all items of expenditure, potential alternatives and ask what would happen if the expenditure was stopped entirely.

Alternative forms of budgeting focus on what are called continuation budgets. These are simply a roll forward of what went in the year before either in absolute terms or with an adjustment for inflation. The problem, particularly in sport, is that these budgets do not encourage growth or tend to be sufficiently flexible to react to market changes. As you will see in Chapters 6 and 7, the sport market is a rapidly changing environment so needs budgets that will be responsive.

HUMAN RESOURCE MANAGEMENT

As we saw in Chapter 3 the management of people is an essential requirement in the sport management sector. Just to reiterate, the reason why the HR function received a specific chapter is because this was the area where much of the early management theory focused on. We covered the main concepts of management earlier but it is worth a quick examination of human resource management here, given its importance as an area of functional management which works alongside marketing and finance. Any organisation serious about success needs to think carefully about how they manage people. This will involve you in a decision-making process, built on good finance of course, that links your organisation's

BOX 4.2   WHO SHOULD SET PRICES: MARKETERS OR ACCOUNTANTS?

We mentioned earlier that functions have, historically at least, often been left to work in isolation. Marketers do the marketing; accountants do the finances and so on. But what about the setting of prices? There is an old discussion about the extent that the price of a product or service should be left to the accountants. In theory, what price is charged should be based on calculating all the costs involved in the development of a product or service, with the price set being one which can cover the costs, plus, if necessary, any profit (there are plenty of different pricing strategies so we've just used a crude one here).

What we need to remember when it comes to sport though is that for a number of organisations the objectives remain not-for-profit. They deliver sport development, society and participation objectives. In an attempt to demonstrate this we use a simple example relating to how a price may be arrived at for a costing of a five-day children's multi-sport holiday camp, run by a community trust:

- Total staff costs £1,800 (4 coaches x £15 pay rate x 6 hours x 5 days)
- Promotional materials £200
- Equipment £25 (£200 spent on equipment but divided by the planned 8 weeks of holiday programmes that the equipment will be used or depreciated over the year)
- Other (e.g. Insurance): £100 (depreciated across activities)
- Total costs: £2,125 operational costs for the week.

In order to work out a possible price to charge children, it can be worthwhile considering what would need to be charged just to cover expenditure. To do this one needs to know the maximum number of children who can do the activities, which can be governed by both regulation, good practice and ensuring and good-quality experience. In this instance the ratio is 15 children per group. Using this information, one possible break-even price (BEP) could be:

- 4 groups x 15 = 60 children (£2, 125 divided by 60) = £36 per child for a week of activities which would cover the cost.

It is often recommended however, that one does not calculate price to a 100 per cent utilisation rate, as people will often drop out at short notice. One common utilisation rate to use 80 per cent. Using this rate will give a different potential BEP:

- 4 groups x 15 = 48 children (80% of 60) (£2, 125 divided by 48) = £43 per child for a week of activities which would cover the cost.

So what price should be charged? Here, these financial calculations can be informed by other considerations. If the trust wants to use it as an additional source of revenue, they could add an additional percentage on the price (cost plus pricing), such as 10 per cent (making the weekly price of £47.30) to help generate a surplus (which if they exceed the 80 per cent utilisation rate can also mean more surplus is generated), which they could then use to support other social activities. But it may not end here. Consideration could be given to what competitors may charge for a similar activity. It could also depend on the type of area, such as if it is a poor or a relatively affluent community. If it is in a poor community and an additional subsidy is given, then the price could in fact be much lower and it could be run as a loss leader, but justified because it helps achieve social objectives. Finally, one could also consider the other possible costs which may remain hidden and less easy to calculate, such as energy costs of the building, or even the administration of the programme.

What this in fact shows is that increasingly it is a not a simple question of a different business function specialist deciding on the price, or being more important, rather that there needs to be understanding and blending of the roles: someone in marketing cannot afford to ignore the cost implications of the price they may decide on; someone in accounts cannot afford to ignore the market and staffing implications of the price they may decide on.

objectives to operational practices. These practices need to be clear, well-planned and realistic to meet the needs of the organisation and its employees.

The best organisations tend to have a HRM philosophy which is underpinned by employee development, encompassing the training and development needs of employees. It is also characterised by a number of the following concepts:

- HRM is generally initiated and facilitated by senior management (remember the hierarchies we examined earlier in the book?);
- line management (the management of smaller groups of staff) are centrally involved in the delivery of the HRM strategy (this helps with the alignment of strategic/operational/project/personal goals);
- HRM policies will outline the relationships between organisational, team and individual objectives (see point above);
- HRM strategies are designed to support, foster and reinforce organisational culture;
- in an effective HRM system the focus is on manager–employee relationships as opposed to management–trade union relations (this is a major reason behind the emergence of the new HRM literature, explained briefly after this list);
- HRM puts employees at the heart of an organisation's culture and will emphasise the importance of engaging employees in the setting of organisational goals, vision, mission and values; and
- employees, crucially, are seen as assets (something of real worth) to the organisation rather than a simple line on the income and expenditure account, or put more simply, a cost.

It's also worth noting here that HRM is a relatively new concept, certainly in modern literature, following its emergence as a clearer business functional discipline in the 1980s by a number of American academics. It is different to more traditional personnel management as HRM provides a much more strategic approach to managing people by focusing on the workforce itself rather than simply the organisational outputs. Whether this approach is new or not (and trust us, many are still debating the origins of HRM) the functions of HRM are essential when running an efficient and effective organisation. We'd argue that this is even more important in a sector like sport that is undeniably a people business. Braithwaite (2004) gives a reminder of the importance of the HR to any business and organisation. A key part of any HR strategy means that in order to ensure customer satisfaction, managers should try to ensure customer needs, brands and staff commitment are synchronised, so this needs contented and satisfied staff. Something easier said than done.

For the detailed overview of HRM and related functions you need to go back and read through Chapter 3, but to complement what we have already put together, here are a few additional key concepts which can be considered in relation to the HR function:

- *Recruitment and selection:* this is a critical role of the HR function whereby methods need to be designed to advertise jobs, develop appropriate selection methods, ranging from tests, interviews or presentations, which will then allow them to be recruited to the organisations.
- *Legal compliance:* increasingly there are many regulations which organisations, whatever the sector, will need to comply with. These can range from health and safety legislation, equal opportunities, holiday entitlements and pay and hours directives.
- *Job design:* this relates to the many motivational theories highlighted in Chapter 3, whereby how you design jobs can impact on motivation, which in turn can affect productivity, or crucially in the service sector, the quality of customer care in the service encounter.
- *Staff appraisal systems:* appraisal systems have become increasingly important in many organisations and are intimately related to quality-control systems. In essence it is about designing systems which can help identify needs, explain organisational goals and establish personal goals and any training needs.

- *Training staff:* developing ways to train both paid and voluntary staff (of which in the sport sector, there are many) is crucial. Training can involve in-house training, or training with external agencies, which can all help in staff motivation and the quality of service delivered.
- *Salaries, payments:* this is another crucial function, which will overlap with the finance function, but having an awareness of any key regulations, such as minimum wage and holiday directives is crucial.

CONCLUSION

So this chapter has explored three of the key business functions which underpin all business activities, which can revolve around the critical areas of staff, money and customers. These business functions are distinguished from the management functions, in that all the management functions need to be applied to these business functional areas.

These business functions have now become highly developed areas, which in relation to degree courses will have many more detailed modules to support their application. It should however be appreciated that whilst in the past, for many large organisations, or even for the convenience of teaching, these areas would be treated separately, the general trend is that contemporary sport managers need to have an understanding of all these areas when making decisions. This helps to prevent a silo mentality developing in people in the organisation, together with encouraging managers to adopt a more holistic approach in their decision-making, whereby the broader implications of their decisions are considered in a variety of areas.

5

THE LEVELS OF MANAGEMENT

INTRODUCTION

So far in this book, we have shown you how sport management roles can be categorised by the functions of management, (discussed in Chapters 1 and 3), the business functions focused on, (discussed in Chapters 1, 3 and 4), and later we will discuss the sector worked in (Chapter 6). In this chapter, we consider another way for analysing and reflecting on sport management roles, which relate to the levels of management. By exploring these levels of management further insight can be gained about the type of work that you may have to do, alongside how a sport management career may develop.

There are a variety of ways that the levels of management can be defined, but for the purposes of this 'Basics' book we focus on three key areas: the operational, the project and the strategic level. Whilst each level is given a separate discussion, care should be taken about applying the categories too rigidly, or viewing the work done at these levels, too separately. Indeed, it should be appreciated that it is more than possible for a single manager to operate at all three levels, whereby they have to ensure the day-to-day operations take place to deliver goods and services on time, whilst they may also have to engage with more specific projects and make plans to achieve long-term strategic objectives.

One of the key themes which will be emphasised as part of the discussion of the strategic level is the importance of understanding the business environment, which (as explained in Chapter 2) is becoming characterised by a greater pace of change and complexity. Today's sport managers must handle these changes, attempting to develop innovative solutions to problems, whilst also ensuring that resources are utilised as efficiently and effectively as possible. The result is that whilst maintaining the day-to-day operations of a facility or organisation is still vital, the need to not only deal with change, but to also try to excel, means that more contemporary work practices are becoming both project- and strategically orientated.

THE LEVELS OF MANAGEMENT: AN OVERVIEW

There are many ways to represent the levels of management within an organisation. One common and simple way to represent the levels is to present them in a hierarchical pyramid as Figure 5.1 illustrates.

Whilst there are a number of variations in relation to the terminology used to refer to the layers of management, the diagram highlights the most common representation of the layers, which are the strategic (top), tactical (middle)

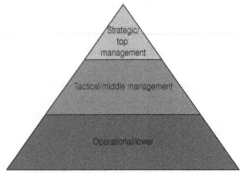

Figure 5.1   Representing the levels of management (classic)

and operational (lower). It is possible to transpose this broad representation of the levels to an organisational hierarchical flow chart (such as those presented in Chapter 3 and particularly for the Nike example). At the top of the pyramid there are a small number of senior executives, or CEOs, who focus on the overall strategic direction, leading the organisation, and setting goals many years in advance. As we move down the pyramid, managers will take more responsibility for the delivery of the strategic plans developed by senior managers, with these middle-level managers perhaps assuming a regional manager role, or someone who manages a specific sport facility or gym. The use of the term 'tactical' level is used in some text books, instead of the term 'middle', whereby the tactical level in essence refers to the methods used to deliver strategies. Finally, the operational level refers to the people who are actually responsible for delivering the overall strategic vision with finished goods and services.

The problem with this simple representation is that it does not, at least not very often, reflect the organisational structure or scale of many sport organisations. For some sport manufacturers, sport clubs and governing bodies this representation can work, but for smaller sport organisations and clubs, whether they operate in the public, private or voluntary sector, they are too small for this common representation to be meaningful. Quite simply, whilst big organisations will have a sufficient number of managers who work at these levels, many sport organisations do not, where there may only be a single manager or a sole entrepreneur. It is like comparing Manchester United FC, or Real Madrid FC, with a small non-league football club; whilst all these clubs will have to consider operational and strategic levels of planning, for the larger clubs, they are likely to have separate, designated management roles, whilst for the small non-league club, the roles will be amalgamated into a limited group of people, even just one person.

Whilst the classic levels model may have many limitations as a representation of an actual organisational structure, it is still relevant in relation to describing the type of work which has to be done, whether this is by one person, or hundreds. For example, for a small to medium-sized sport organisation, this can mean that it is perfectly possible for a manager, or the head of a club, to consider strategic and governance issues and operational issues as part of their management duties.

Into this mix of the operational and the strategic management levels can go the project level. Project management is not usually represented as a level, but a discrete, separate part of management. The reason it is given more prominence here (in this book), is because it is increasingly evident that managers operating at both a strategic and operational level have to engage more with projects and their management, not only to deal with change, but also to try to make their sport, their organisation, or their service stand out and excel. This is particularly relevant in relation to sport events and fundraising projects. Furthermore, as was highlighted in Chapter 1 and the examples of jobs, the area of project management can overlap with both the project and the strategic levels of management, such as the years of planning needed to stage a large-scale sporting event, then all the operational issues which must be considered when it is delivered.

For these reasons, the preference in this chapter is to use the term 'levels of management' to refer to the operational and the management levels, substituting the 'middle' or 'tactical' level with the project level. As will be explained later, while each of these levels overlap, they can require the use of different management skills and particularly the use of different analytical tools, even at times, different ways of thinking. This is why the project level in Figure 5.2 is represented as flowing from the strategic level, but bisecting the operational level. What this means is that projects, such as bidding for a large-scale sport event, need to be planned for at a strategic level many years in advance. As the event date approaches, the management level will be more operational focused, as the management of the event focuses on the day-to-day activities which need to be done in order to stage a successful event.

The final point to consider is how these levels of management relate to the five key management functions discussed in Chapters 1 and 3. To illustrate how these different

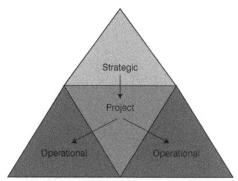

Figure 5.2   Representing the levels of management (preferred)

management functions are applied at the different levels and some of the variations which may occur, these are summarised and compared in Table 5.1. It should also be appreciated that the business functions discussed in the previous chapter can also be performed at the different levels of management, as Figure 4.1 in Chapter 4, illustrated. These different levels will be explored further in the subsequent sections.

OPERATIONAL LEVEL OF MANAGEMENT

Operational management is, essentially, about producing and delivering services or goods. We can point to a variety of different definitions that may add additional elements to this basic definition, for example McMahon-Beattie and Yeoman (2004 p. 28), add that this delivery should be done *effectively* (i.e. a good or service that delivers and meets people's needs and quality expectations) and *efficiently* (the maximum output, such as the number of users or revenue generated, in relation to the resource input, such as staff used). One can also add to this definition of operational management, that these services or goods must be delivered safely and meet the quality standards set, within the prescribed budgets, at a designated time.

Definitions of operational management often refer to how it is a process which is about 'transforming inputs into outputs' (Heizer and Render 2004 p. 4). This perhaps betrays the strong roots that much operational management theory

Table 5.1   Comparing management functions at the different levels of management

Levels of management		
Operational	*Project*	*Strategic*
Plan		
In terms of the timescales that are planned for, these will vary from immediate, on-the-spot decisions, to planning hours, days or months in advance. An essential part of operational management will always be the breaking down of job tasks in order to help track who is, or should be doing what, when, where and how.	The timescales that are planned for can vary between operational timescales of days and months, particularly during the final implementation and completion of the project, to the strategic timescales of years, such as the lengthy time processes needed to initially put in a bid for a large-scale or mega-sporting event.	The timescales dealt with at a strategic level relate to a year, three years and even up to fifteen years, but with such strategic plans likely to need key revisions as the business environment changes. The assessment of the business environment is a critical part of the analysis which needs to underpin the plan.
Organise		
In terms of the breadth of resources which are organised, such as the number of staff who are managed these may be fewer in number unless the role is of a senior operational management role in the manufacturing sector. Generally, a manager working at an operational level, may for example be responsible for just one facility, which is contrasted with the strategic level, where they may oversee a number of facilities.	An essential part of project management is keeping track of schedules and deadlines. This is the area of deciding who is doing what, when, where and how again, along with ensuring other resources, such as time and money, are secured.	Here the broad organisational goals and objectives are identified, such as how much profit they may want to generate in future years, or demand and usage figures for the participation in sport. These objectives could then be broken down at an operational level, such as monthly targets of income or usage.
Lead		
Staff must have confidence in the manager, particularly if it is in relation to crisis and risk situations, where decisions have to be made in response to the immediate, dynamic conditions faced.	The project manager is the focal point, or the hub for bringing together group effort, but may not necessarily be the most senior manager in the organisation, but can still lead others.	This is critical, because the senior managers and the head or CEO has, as illustrated in Mintzberg's roles (illustrated in Chapter 3), an important representative or figurehead role. How they appear, perform and

Levels of management		
Operational	Project	Strategic
		communicate can have a critical role in setting the tone of the organisational culture and staff motivation.

Control

It is about checking that all the key inputs are in place to ensure a service can take place, along with monitoring performance, such as attendance levels for activities and considering if actions should be put in place to deal with any problems.	It is crucial that the schedules of work deadlines are tracked, particularly if the work has been delegated. The importance of monitoring and keeping track of work really cannot be stressed enough, as Box 5.2 illustrates, where if one piece of work is missed, it can mean a whole project is jeopardised.	In large organisations, senior managers will control a number of managers, trying to ensure that strategies are implemented and worked out at an operational level. For small organisations, monitoring and controlling performance may mean that a manager may, for example look at monthly operational performances, and then project that performance into the future.

Communicate

This can relate to both staff and customers, as operational managers often have a crucial direct contact point with customers. It is vital that they can effectively communicate to all people involved, for example, dealing effectively with customer complaints.	Project managers potentially need to utilise many forms of communication. If it is a small project, then the manager will have to take care of all the business functional areas, relating to finance, marketing and HR themselves; if it is a larger project, these may be broken down and delegated into designated roles, where communication is of critical importance between those who have the work delegated to them and keeping track of work.	This can relate to communicating to managers, key stakeholders and being the public face of an organisation. It may mean that how they communicate and to whom they communicate, may be different from those managers working at the operational level. The temptation may be to see communication simply flowing down the hierarchy, but as explained in Chapter 3 there are many logistical and moral dangers with this approach.

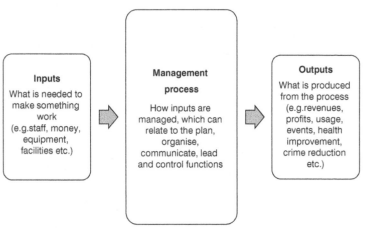

Figure 5.3   A simple operational management system

has in the manufacturing industries, but it is still useful to use the imagery of representing an organisation as a system, which needs inputs to get it to work, such as money and people, which are then combined in a process to produce outputs, such as usage, revenue and profit. A summary of these key elements of a management system are represented in Figure 5.3. It is useful to recognise the terms of inputs and outputs, as they can often be used in textbooks and when describing job tasks in job advertisements.

Operational management then is about managing processes, which involves people and other resources (i.e. the inputs), in order to achieve some tangible outcome, such as people participating in a sport, or generating profits (i.e. the outputs). It is about, for example, a duty manager of a sport facility or gym dealing with the day-to-day issues of running a sport facility, which can involve obvious tasks, such as: ensuring the facility opens and closes on time; staff are where they should be; safety practices are adhered to; customers are dealt with; and numerous potential issues, which can range from accidents, machines breaking down, theft of belongings, or a customer feeling they have experienced a poor service. These must all be dealt with and managed in order to ensure the facility continues to operate, which in turn helps ensure the organisational objectives are achieved, whether these relate to profit, or simply encouraging people to participate in sport to achieve some less tangible social objectives.

In Chapter 3 we outlined how effective management is underpinned by time management. At its root this starts with breaking down a job into tasks or nested elements. From this process of identifying the many subtasks which have to be done to complete a task, the basis of an operational checklist is established, as Box 5.1 illustrates. The simplest way of beginning a checklist is to start by asking the basic questions of management, based around who, what, why, when, where and how. This helps identify what needs to be done. Some of these checklists will be done to track work, whilst others are done before an activity or task is engaged with, such as the safety procedural checklist illustrated in Box 5.1.

To further illustrate the sort of work a sport manager working at the operational level would do, here are two real examples of operational based jobs, with some of the key concept highlighted in Table 5.2.

BOX 5.1   PRODUCING OPERATIONAL CHECKLISTS

Checklists, whilst sometimes appearing obvious, simplistic even, and so not worthy of serious management thinking, should in fact form a foundation for operational and, indeed, project management. Their use forms a critical underpinning in total quality management (TQM), which refers to the idea that if strict procedures are adhered to, then this can help ensure that the product or service is delivered to a set quality. A quality product, it should be emphasised, is not necessarily about producing goods and services which are expensive; it is about the product or service meeting the expectations of customers. This is a critical part of manufacturing, where there is an attempt avoid any mistakes in the manufacturing process, whereby the cost of rectifying a mistake (such as a product recall) is far more costly than trying to prevent the problem occurring in the first instance. To do this, quality checklists are developed at every stage of the production process to ensure that, to use the common adage of quality management, a good quality product is delivered first time, every time.

Of course, one of the characteristics of a service is its variability, whereby the human factor and the elements of the unknown mean it can be difficult to achieve the same quality output every time. So does this mean quality operational checklists have no use in sport management? Of course not. Checklists can be vital in relation to safety procedures, in much the same way a pilot will always systematically adhere to the checklist before a take-off, or a surgeon will go through a checklist before an operation. For example, the following checklists may be designed by a manager, in conjunction with their sport coaches, which the coaches must do before any activity, whereby they would do the following checks:

- Are coaches qualified and police checked?
- Is there someone who is first aid qualified?
- Has parent/guardian completed contact details?
- Has a medical history form been completed, identifying any medical problems?
- Has a register been taken?
- Has the pitch been inspected before the activity?
- Has coach checked child's safety equipment (e.g. gum shields, pads, helmets etc.)?
- Have they warmed up and stretched?
- Do they have drinks?

A manager when designing operational checklists should aim to get them on one sheet of paper, which are easy to scan and read, together with developing a culture where they are systematically used. If these checklists of actions are adhered to then, as noted earlier, this can prevent an accident or incident occurring which can have potentially profound implications for the participants, the staff and ultimately the credibility and viability of the organisation.

Table 5.2   Comparing different operational jobs

Job 1 – Health development officer

A job relating to a health development officer had the remit of designing and delivering sport programmes to help improve health through sport or active recreation programmes. It is of interest that having experience of project management was also desirable. In terms of the key skills stated, these related to having excellent time management, interpersonal, written and verbal communication skills, along with having the technical subject knowledge relating to sport and health development.

Job 2 – Operational sport facility manager

A job for a general manager for the Xercise4less group who manage a number of sport and finesses facilities, involved the day-to-day running of a club safely and efficiently. It is operational in focus as it also involved implementing business plans to achieve revenue targets, whilst also responsible for managing the sales, membership and recruitment of staff. Interestingly, one of their criteria was that they were looking for an experienced general manager who is 'obsessed with staying connected to the detail, operating at all levels and no job beneath them', which is a call for a hands-on manager. In terms of skills required, these ranged from operations and sales, leadership, influencing skills and commercial acumen and managing revenue streams.

PROJECT LEVELS OF MANAGEMENT

O'Conell (1996) describes a project as:

> like a journey: it involves identifying a destination, setting out, travelling and ending up somewhere; hopefully the place you intended to be.
>
> (O'Conell, 1996, p2)

This illustrates some of the key distinguishing features of project management, in comparison with the other levels of management. Using Nicholas's (2001) definition with some additional elements, project management has the following key features:

- there must be a clear purpose or be goal-directed;
- it is non-routine from usual management functions and has a uniqueness to the work;
- be a temporary activity with a clear end point or timescales;
- will have elements of unfamiliarity;
- and have a stake such as in relation to finance, time or reputation.

What can actually constitute a sport project can be incredibly varied. It may relate to organising an event, or initiating a fundraising campaign, or even supervising the development of a new sport facility. Whilst some of the technical knowledge or skills may vary from these different projects, they will still need to utilise the basic generic management functions and skills which act as a foundation, but then will also need to utilise more specific tools designed for project management (e.g. using project management software to help with the management function of controlling and monitoring work).

Understanding, identifying and managing timescales is a crucial underpinning in any project. To help convey how a project will vary over its life span (remember, a key distinguishing feature of a project is that it must be goal-directed and have a clear end point), projects are often said to go through a lifecycle. Burke (1999, p. 28), for example, identifies four key stages in the lifecycle, which are represented here, but illustrated with a sport example:

- *Concept:* from team meetings, a decision is made for a sport facility to stage a large sport community festival, to build links with the community, expand membership and try and get younger people involved in sports.
- *Development/definition:* a plan is outlined, identifying the date when the event will take place, then from that point, clearly specifying the purpose and what needs to be done, by whom, by when and how. For the community sport festival, a decision is made on the locations, dates and variety of programmes which will take place.
- *Implementation/execution:* people have to carry out or execute all the job tasks identified in the plan. Issues of scheduling (the order that job tasks are done) are of critical importance here, because if one job is not done, then the whole project may grind to a halt. For the festival, key stakeholders are contacted, such as the police and schools, along with organising training schedules for volunteers, booking equipment and checking all staff are briefed.
- *Termination:* once the event is done, that is not necessarily the end of the work, as it is usually necessary to conduct

some post-event evaluation, thank people for their involvement, check that invoices are paid, etc. For the sport festival this can involve press releases, newsletters and evaluation reports, some of which may involve monitoring participation data for months or years after the event to try and gauge its full impact.

As with operational management a key starting point will always be the identification of tasks and sub-tasks (sometimes called nested processes), a process which forms the key bedrock of good management. From this basic starting point, projects often utilise a variety of more specific technical skills and tools, together with perhaps requiring a technical knowledge of the sport area the project focuses on, such as knowing which funds to access for a fundraising project. Here are a few of the more specific project-planning concepts and tools which would have to be utilised:

- *Project management software and training:* there a number of pieces of software which can be used to help manage projects, such as, among others, Microsoft Project. Another example of a project management approach is PRINCE2 (which stands for PRojects IN Controlled Environments), which offers a variety of project management services, ranging from training and process downloads and is used by a wide range of large companies and governments. It also offers qualifications, which may be specified in some project management jobs.
- *Scheduling and milestones:* scheduling begins with the basic management job of a manager to identify the tasks and sub-tasks of a job which needs to be done. It is then absolutely essential that the manager next considers the order or the sequence that these jobs must be done, or the schedule. For example, the tasks and sub-tasks identified for promoting an event could be: task – producing a promotional leaflet (examples of sub-tasks relate to designing a leaflet; reviewing and proofreading it; printing it; picking it up and distributing it); task – write press (examples of sub-tasks relate to collecting information, talking to people, sending

it in etc.). Obviously, the first key milestone to put in place is the date when the project must be completed, such as the date of the event, or the closing date for funding bids. Other milestones can help keep schedules on track and help review performance and direction.   An example of the critical importance of scheduling and keeping track of who does what, when where and how is given in Box 5.2.

- *Gantt charts:* Gantt charts are a way of visually representing the key tasks, their relationships, milestones and the scheduling of the work. The scale of the project can influence the number of resources and people which need to be coordinated. Indeed, it is perfectly feasible for a sport manager to engage with a project without having to coordinate other people, or delegate any tasks. More usually however a project will need a team of people, which means that there will have to be a project leader, which may or may not be a sport manager, but will certainly need to employ the key management functions and skills.

Furthermore, at times the distinctions between project management and operational management can become very blurred. A manager may discover that as part of their operational 'to-do' working checklists, it will mix both the operational tasks (e.g. ensuring a facility is clean, goods are ordered, staff are paid, complaints are dealt with, correspondence replied to etc.), which may be blended with the tasks necessary to complete a project (e.g. writing letters to potential sponsors, sending out the letters, etc.). This can be challenging and will certainly test the skills of management, but which, it must be reiterated, is vital for a sport manager to engage with in order to stay viable and competitive, whether this is for an event, funding bids, or new facilities.

To further illustrate the sort of work a sport manager working at the project level would do, here are two real examples of project-based jobs, with some of the key concepts highlighted in Table 5.3.

BOX 5.2 THE IMPORTANCE OF KEEPING TRACK OF WORK AND THE RISKS WHEN YOU FAIL TO DO THIS

There is a classic old rhyme or proverb which reminds us about the importance of sequencing work, and how forgetting one small, seemingly unimportant detail, can have profound implications. There are many variations, with no single authoritative author, but in essence it runs as:

> For want of a nail, the shoe was lost.
> For want of a shoe the horse was lost.
> For want of a horse the rider was lost.
> For want of a rider the battle was lost.
> For want of a battle the kingdom was lost.
> And all for the want of a horseshoe nail.

What does this have to do with sport and project management? It offers a simple way to illustrate the necessity of not overlooking a small detail and the importance of scheduling, where if one small detail is missed, the whole project can be jeopardised. An example of the metaphorical nail can be illustrated with the example of the Sheffield half marathon being cancelled in 2014. The event seemed to be well-managed and run, having good publicity with thousands turning out to both participate and watch. Roads had been closed and runners were ready on the starting line, when it was announced that the race had to be cancelled. The reason for the cancellation was because the water suppliers had not turned up with bottled water, so the event organisers felt that the risks to runners were too great to allow the event to continue. This decision, based on the risk to runners, was a fair and reasonable one to make (reflect on what the consequences would have been if someone had collapsed and died, which may have been linked to a lack of water). The critical question to ask is why was there no water on the day of the event, when every other detail of the event was in place and seemed to be working well? It turned out that the reason the water was not supplied was because the suppliers had not been paid, despite having sent a number of invoices and reminders to the event organisers. Somewhere, someone in the organisation had not tracked this simple task, which raises some crucial questions about the effectiveness of the delegation, leadership, controls and communication. The ramifications of this relatively simple task of ensuring that the invoice was dealt with and payment sent was profound: for the want of a payment, the supplier was lost. For the want of the supplier, the race was cancelled. For the want of the event, the reputation was lost. And with this loss, the business was lost. All for the want of an invoice not dealt with!

Table 5.3 Project-based jobs

Job 1 – Sport project event-management company in Brazil

A specialist Brazilian sports and entertainment agency (iLUKA) advertised for a job focusing on large-scale event planning, and advertised for a senior event manager. The role focused on project managing events for clients, from the initial planning, right up to their operational delivery. The work would include the management of budgets and coordinating key stakeholders in major events. The focus on larger-scale events would mean it had a more strategic focus in terms of the breadth of resources and timescales which would have to be managed. Interestingly, in terms of experience, it was specified that at least five years working in sport events and/or experiential marketing (see Chapter 7), along with experience of managing budgets, resources, sport organisations and finally being bilingual in English and Portuguese.

Job 2 – Project event and development manager for the IPC

As part of the International Paralympic Committee (IPC) a job of an athletics project manager was advertised. The work involved managing and coordination the planning processes for IPC athletic competitions and events, along with monitoring and reporting on complex project planning, follow-up tasks and milestones. The work would also involve liaising with many different groups and athletes (i.e. the key stakeholders), along with conducting day-to-day administrative activities. In terms of requirements, a relevant university degree in business or sport management was required, along with experience in project planning and event management. There was also the need to have a proven ability to meet deadlines (i.e. time management), strong analytical skills and be a good communicator.

STRATEGIC LEVEL OF MANAGEMENT

It is common for books on strategy to highlight the military roots of the word, which was initially used to refer to the art of controlling armies and military campaigns, which could involve a large and complex coordination of resources. Not surprisingly, this challenge of coordination and planning large-scale resources was one viewed as applicable to the management of large-scale organisations, hence its transfer into the language of business. Johnson *et al* (2008, p. 12), have produced a number of key books identifying the key features of strategic management as referring to:

- the need to understand the strategic position of the organisation;
- making strategic choices for the future; and
- managing strategy in action.

Distilling the key elements from a variety of writers who define strategy, the following key features can be identified in relation to strategic management:

- it is about trying to envision a future in terms of where the organisation wants to be;
- it is about identifying medium- to long-term aims, goals or objectives, which should be measurable;
- it is about adapting to the changing business environment and seeing how the organisation can respond effectively to those changes, seizing the opportunities, or dealing with the threats.

Furthermore, a key part of many definitions of strategy refers to the importance of identifying positions, making choices and managing strategies in response to changes in the different layers of the business environment. There are three commonly cited layers of the environment, which are:

- *The internal environment:* this refers to the actual organisation itself, which it has more control over. The strengths and weaknesses of a SWOT analysis usually focus on this level, as illustrated in Box 5.3.
- *The external business environment:* this refers to those areas which the organisation has little to no control over, often organised around the categories of PEST factors, with some adding legal and the natural environment layers, to make PESTLE (see Box 5.3). It can also consider the opportunities and threats as part of a SWOT analysis.

BOX 5.3   AN EXAMPLE OF A SWOT AND PEST ANALYSIS

SWOT and PEST are perhaps two of the most common techniques to try and assess how changes may affect a business. A SWOT analysis refers to an organisation reviewing its internal strengths and weaknesses, then considering what opportunities and threats may exist, which usually focus on the external business environment. More refinement to   the opportunities and threats analysis can be had by organising the analysis around the political, economic, social, technological environment (PEST) factors. Hopefully, the key potential drivers of change are identified, which will create a variety of opportunities and threats (or risks) to the organisation, a number of which were illustrated in Chapter 2.

The following examples relate to a simplified SWOT and PEST which a local government produced for its sport and leisure services.

Strengths	Weaknesses
Committed staff.	Restricted revenue for reinvestment.
Skilled and qualified staff.	Political impediments and council
Qualified pool of volunteers.	indecision.
Good brand and reputation.	Inconsistent use of new social
Commitment to safety.	media and technology.
Trust in education sport related	Ageing sporting infrastructure.
services.	Need to strengthen organisational
	culture and purpose of services.

Usually, an additional opportunity and threat grid would also be considered. However, in this instance, the threats and opportunities were framed around the PEST factors. As you look at some of the examples highlighted under PEST consider how they can be considered as either threats or opportunities.

Political	Economic
VAT and taxation changes.	Rising utility/energy costs for sport
Central government policies of	facilities.
austerity reducing available funds.	Rising unemployment and welfare
Funding to government sport	costs.
agencies cut.	Financial controls.
Duty bound for protecting statutory	Regional industries decline.
services (e.g. education, health etc.).	Failure to secure external funding
Green and health agenda.	based on population density.
Election – new government with	Need to attract businesses to
different policies.	relocate.
	Growth in private, branded gyms in
	the region.

Social	Technological
Ageing local population.	Social media.
Obesity.	Updating facility software/
New entertainments.	programming systems.
Growth in HE education sector and	Development of call centres.
sport courses.	
Use of sport to develop social	
capital.	

- *The intermediate environment:* this may refer to competitors, which the organisation may have some control over what they may do, such as initiating a price cut to try to be competitive.

Identifying how changes stemming from the business environment can affect a sport business is regarded as an important part of a marketing plan and a central part of the more encompassing process of strategic planning. If these changes are not identified, then appropriate actions and strategies cannot be put in place, which in turn may mean the future viability of the organisation may be threatened. Using SWOT and PEST(LE) techniques offer a simple, easy-to-use starting point, which can be further complemented by the use of additional models and theories. Whatever tool, model or theory used, the crucial point to appreciate is that these are designed to help the manager in their conceptual management skills, which can then be used for the basis of producing a strategic plan and more specific strategies to manage the change and ensure the long-term viability of the organisation.

Whilst the core management functions and skills discussed in Chapters 3 and 4 will be needed, they will be focused on some specific considerations which a manager working at a strategic level will have to consider, such as:

- *Developing strategic plans:* strategic management is different from strategic planning. Producing a strategic plan in theory should establish where the organisation wants to be in the future, such as market position, its key market segments it focuses on, if it is to change direction, or even develop new services and products through diversification of its sport services or products. As part of this identification of where the organisation wants to be in the future, an outline of some of the strategies for how to achieve the future goals will be needed.

- *Developing mission statements:* a mission statement should try to clearly define the purpose or essence of a business, or organisation in a few sentences. Good mission statements should be market-orientated (see Chapter 4), whereby the sport service or good is defined in relation to how it meets customers' needs and wants. (The importance of this means it is returned to in Chapter 7.) Not everyone advocates the use of mission statements, or regards them as important, but engaging with the process to try and write one in relation to identifying what the organisation is there for can offer many potential benefits.

To further illustrate the sort of work a sport manager working at the strategic level would do, two real examples of sport strategic management jobs, with some of the key concepts highlighted, are presented in Table 5.4.

THE IMPORTANCE OF GOVERNANCE

In the past, many non-commercial sport organisations, such as the governing bodies of sport, could be organised and managed in a very ad-hoc, often chaotic manner. The voluntary nature of the organisations could mean that they could be run by interested volunteers, who may have been self-interested, or approach the work in relation to preserving the sport as they experienced it in the past, not necessarily what it should be in the future. As the many examples used in Chapter 2 illustrated, the governing bodies of sport were often forces of conservatism, where they could be slow to respond to the social, economic and technological changes taking place in the business environment.

Today, having such ad-hoc arrangements is no longer viable for many sport organisations. What one has seen is that

Table 5.4   Examples of sport strategic management jobs

Job 1 – Local authority strategic project manager

A programme manager for a district council focused on the area of strategic project management. In essence the role involved transforming the leisure facilities for the district (so it is strategic in the breadth of resources or facilities which would have to be coordinated) over a two- to three-year period (so also strategic in its timescales). The role needed to have an understanding of financial management and operational management in the design of service specifications, along with developing a variety of new and ongoing sport and leisure projects. Part of the skill set needed related to having experience of project management and the technical skills relating to funding. One of the requirements was the ability to use the PRINCE2 project management framework.

Job 2 – Unpaid strategic executive role for a governing body of sport

A very different type of job was advertised for a voluntary independent board member for British Weight Lifting. The person would sit as a member on the independent governing board, which was seeking people to contribute to the strategic development and growth in both recreational and professional weightlifting. As part of this role on the board, it would mean they had responsibility for ensuring that the governing body fulfilled their corporate objectives, meeting the expectations of the key stakeholders and running the organisation on a sound financial footing. As well as giving the strategic insight, the role involved attending board meetings, reviewing and monitoring performance in relation to the corporate objectives and keeping up-to-date with current developments. What is of interest is how it is a voluntary position, but it is a position which carries great authority and operates at a strategic level.

all sport organisations must be managed properly, which is increasingly being framed around the notion of corporate governance. In essence corporate governance relates to the 'structures and systems of control by which managers are held accountable to those who have a legitimate stake in an organisation' (Johnson *et al.* 2008, p. 133). Although the theory and practice of governance is rooted in the management of large commercial corporations, both the theory and the legal regulations which have been put in place to ensure good and effective governance have reverberated far beyond these organisations.

One of the features of good governance is the putting in place of clear strategic plans. This now means that any properly managed sport organisation, whether it operates in the public, voluntary or private sector, must put together a strategic plan. In the private sector, this has been done for a long time. For the other sectors, particularly for many voluntary governing bodies of sport, it has been a more recent issue that they have had to engage with. Not only is it regarded as part of good governance and good business management, but more pragmatically, for the governing bodies of sport, it impacts on the likelihood of receiving money from governments, or their agencies, such as Sport England.

CONCLUSION

Whatever the level of management, a key foundation will always be the need to perform the basic management functions of planning, organising, controlling, leading and communicating. These functions deal with the basic questions of management, which are summarised by the who, what, when, where and how questions any manager needs to ask when approaching any task, in any business function, at any level of management.

From this broad, generic management base, the different levels of management will influence the management timescales dealt with, the scale of the resources coordinated and the need to use or apply different tools and analytical techniques to different situations and problems. Finally, understanding the levels gives a sense of how future careers can develop and what businesses need in the current competitive environment. They show that whilst managers and development officers may begin with operationally based work, in order to try to excel they will need to engage with more innovative projects and have an understanding of strategy. As they progress, it is likely they will be more involved with analysing the business environment in order to think, act and plan strategically.

6

THE SPORT INDUSTRY AND THE BASIS OF PROVISION

INTRODUCTION

It's probably clear by now that the sport industry is fairly significant on a number of levels. We've talked throughout this book about a variety of sport services, events and products; now what needs to be considered is the economic significance of sport and just who provides it. Across the world sport is a multi-trillion dollar industry. Trends in the UK over the latter part of the 1990s and into the new millennium were replicated across the Western world with economic activity rising year on year. Moreover, since the emergence of new global powers such as China, India and Brazil we have seen similar growth in the value of sport in their economies.

The economics of sport traditionally focused on the amount of money involved in the elite level of sport, such as: how much McDonalds pay to sponsor the Olympic Games; how much the newest commercial partner is worth to the Indian Premier League; how much Floyd Mayweather will earn from a boxing match; or how much Fox Sports are prepared to pay to broadcast a major event. Despite this coverage, consumer expenditure – the spending on sport generated by you and us – is not in fact dominated by such payments. Our spending, in the main, consists of expenditure related to participation in sport and on sporting products and services. Collectively this spending can generate substantial economic activity in national and international economies.

But, before we start to look at this in more detail, have you ever wondered who supplies sport goods and services? Whilst the manufacturing of sport goods is primarily provided by private, profit-driven commercial organisations, the provision of sport services and events can be more mixed and will involve other delivery partners, including the state and voluntary sectors. In this chapter, we'll therefore give an explanation of the different types of economic systems and how the provision of sport can be provided by three key sectors: the private, public and voluntary. We explain why different sectors emerge to provide services and how this mix of provision can vary from country to country.

TYPES OF ECONOMIC SYSTEMS

Classic economic theory is founded on studying the problem of how scarce resources are distributed to people throughout a society. Economics deals with the questions of how food, clothes, cars, toys, sport equipment, etc., are distributed and to who and why. Economics deals with the critical questions of why certain organisations, from commercial enterprises to governments, are willing to provide certain goods and services, and what price is charged (if any). All these things are so enmeshed with our everyday lives that we rarely stop to think about how these are done, why they are done and who benefits.

A starting point for understanding the economics of sport is to reflect on how the type of economic system influences what sport products and services are supplied or provided. It is possible to describe three key economic types of systems which deal with the problem of distributing resources in society in different ways, which are:

- *Free-market, capitalist economies:* free-market economic theories deal with the questions of who gets what, where and how by using the free market. In its purest form, a free-market economy relates to private individuals owning property and capital (this essentially describes the machines, factories and workplaces which are used to produce goods and services, which are sometimes called the 'means of production'), whereby the decision to make a product, or provide a service is based on the supplier making a profit on what they sell. This system lays the foundation for some basic key principles of economics which relate to: the price of a good depends on the interaction of supply and demand; if too much is supplied, or demand is not large enough, in theory the price will drop; if too little is supplied, or demand too strong, then the price will rise. When the two are in balance, then price equilibrium is reached. Usually, free-market systems are entwined with the liberal political systems, which means there is a belief in individual freedom and governments should be elected. Whilst there are some who advocate that everything should be left to the free market, when businesses have free rein and are not regulated by governments, this can create many inequalities, social problems and potentially political instability, which ultimately is not healthy for any economic system (see Chapter 2).
- *Command economies:* command economies deal with the question of distributing scarce resources by the state or government deciding who gets what, where, when and how. In their purest form, government or government agencies decide the quantity, design and the price charged for goods. It is a system based on the state, not individuals, owning property and capital, which in theory is managed for the collective benefit of all. In terms of politics, it is usually associated with authoritarian, communist systems, which means there are no free elections, with one party, even person, ruling. The problem with command economies is that they can be overly bureaucratic and inefficient in the distribution of resources, together with reducing freedom of choice, often suffering endemic corruption.

- *Mixed economies:* mixed economic systems distribute resources via both the free market and by government planning and intervention. So for certain goods or services it is possible to see both the free market provide for services, such as with health, education and leisure, which can be financially lucrative, or because these things are deemed to have benefits to all in society, they may also be provided by governments (see later sections for a fuller discussion). Most economies around the world are mixed, as they attempt to deal with the shortcomings of just relying on the free market or economies being centrally planned. It is a mix which varies between democratic mixed economies and authoritarian mixed economies.

The reality is that in the world, apart from a few anomalies such as the communist country of North Korea, most countries' economies would best be described as mixed capitalist economic systems, but it is a mix which has some remarkable variations. These variations are illustrated in Box 6.1 and in the later sections of this chapter. One question which may spring to mind is 'why is it important to understand the type of economic mix provided?' There are two considerations here:

- *Insight into government politics and market threats and opportunities:* certainly in Western capitalist economies, from the USA, UK, Australia, Japan etc. there has been considerably debate as to what extent governments should intervene in the economy, either through the provision of services, or the regulation of business. It has been through various ebbs and flows as to which is the best provider, whereby there tends to be a skew towards using the principles of the free market. Hence over time many industries have been privatised (i.e. where the ownership of an industry is sold back into private ownership), or contracted out (governments and business still retain ownership, such as a sport centre, but the facility is managed for a specified number of years by a commercial company).

- *Supply and demand (the economic mix) provides a basis with which to compare the effectiveness and efficiency of provision of sport*: governments and governing bodies of sport are constantly looking around the world to look at different models for the provision of sport. Sometimes this can be looking at how elite performers are identified and supported to win international events, whilst at other times, it can be about how people should be encouraged to participate more in sport in order to stay healthy. In terms of the latter examples, many countries have attempted to replicate or achieve some of the sport participation rates for the general population of some of the Scandinavian countries, which are often characterised by being more equal societies, have more state intervention and regulation, along with some of the healthiest and active populations in the world.

UNDERSTANDING THE SPORT MARKET

So the distribution of goods such as food and clothing, along with services such as health, education or sport, can depend on the economic mix, which relates to how much the public, voluntary or private sector provide goods or services. All these different examples can be categorised and described as markets. Hence there is a market for food, for health, for education and obviously, sport.

There are many books and articles written about money in sport, indeed this book has covered some of this and will cover more in Chapter 7 and explore the demand for sport. Here, though, we need to focus on how sport is supplied. To do that we first need to work out what the sport market actually is and how it 'broadly' functions.

Many will tend to think of the economics of sport as the analysis of the business of sport or the money in/of sport and there are plenty of easy examples to use to see why: Pepsi and the Indian Premier League; Sky's broadcasting rights deal for the English Premier League; the most expensive advertising space in world television during the NFL Superbowl; not to mention how much we have to pay for a spectator ticket to watch our favourite sports team or athlete. Although this side

BOX 6.1   COMPARING THE USA AND THE CHINESE ECONOMIES AND THE IMPLICATIONS FOR SPORT

Politically, China is still defined as a single-party communist state, which in theory would imply that the economy is centrally controlled and managed for the benefit of all. The reality is far more complex. Whilst politically China may still be seen by many as an authoritarian country which is still categorised as communist in terms of its economic system, we have seen the emergence of change. The Chinese economy has gone through a process of transition, whereby it has moved away from an economic planned approach, to using a more market-based approach. This mix of communism and capitalism is sometimes described as the 'third way'. As a consequence this has meant a great deal of privatisation and deregulation has taken place in China. Interestingly, in terms of sport, despite the underlying principles of communism and its commitment to equality, a greater part of state involvement with sport involves the selection and support of elite athletes, not the masses, as this ties in with the objective of state building.

The USA is the country which perhaps best encapsulates the principles of liberalism and free-market capitalism. Even though it is a capitalist economy, it can still have a surprising amount of government intervention in the economy in terms of spending and regulation in comparison with China. In terms of sport, the role of the federal government is more limited, as indeed it is at a devolved state level. The provision of sport is far more reliant on the private sector, whether this relates to activities done for profit, or private donations. It perhaps explains why there are the interesting examples of how American Winter Olympics team in 2014 supported themselves and their training primarily through sponsorship and charitable donations (BBC 2014).

of the market is interesting, and we will come back to it, we need to point out that while this money is growing, it does in fact make up only a small proportion of the total sport market.

A focus on the elite level of sport has been obvious for two reasons. First, it is because it has strong media appeal in terms of the drama of the sport stories, or the lives of the athletes.

Second, the numbers are easy to identify because most professional sports publish accounts so we can calculate the value of deals quite easily. What is more difficult is quantifying the expenditure on sport in a country as a whole, as there are so many avenues for expenditure and activity can be much more recreational in context. Gratton and Taylor (2000) give us a useful reference point here when they illustrated the hierarchical nature of the sport market. Figure 6.1 provides visual confirmation that while the elite end of the sport market is important, it is much, much smaller than the mass participation market. At the top of the pyramid you find a group of top athletes competing in national and international competitions. Money will flow 'in' to this area via sponsorship, paying spectators and from television companies etc. Towards the bottom we find people, (probably) like us, in the mass-participation sector who are part of the sport market because they want to have fun or get fitter, or both. There will often be some form of government subsidy here via a provision of facilities or through other subsidy to reduce prices, while the voluntary sector will be active in supporting mass participation events such as 10k fun runs and the like. There will also be lots of spending on sport here – from travel for things like skiing holidays, to sports equipment and clothing so that you can participate with some level of appropriate attire.

We can see clearly from Figure 6.1 that there is significant government and voluntary sector involvement throughout the pyramid, where there are large flows of money from the mass-participation market to the commercial providers through expenditure on sports clothing and equipment, private gyms and so on. What you are also hopefully seeing here is a more complex picture for the delivery of sport that extends much further than elite sport. You should be able to see a supply side of the sport market which involves a unique mix of public, private and voluntary sector providers and it's important that we cover each of those in turn in the remainder of this chapter. The supply side can vary from country to country.

In the past, during the 1980s, it was easier to distinguish between each of the sector providers as each had a clearly defined role; governments would provide sport facilities

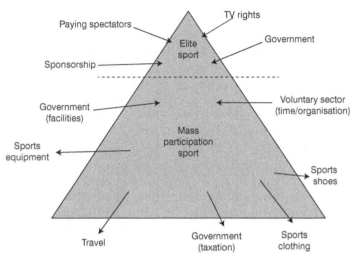

Figure 6.1   The sport market

and subsidise activities, the voluntary sector would run local sports clubs and the private sector would look after professionalised sport and those with sufficient disposable income to use private member clubs. Each sector had different users and therefore different ways to satisfy their needs. However, by the 1990s the lines between the three sectors started to become a little less clear. Local sport clubs, for example, were run by volunteers but would often need to use government (public) facilities to play and train in and would try to find sponsorship from the private sector. If we extend this example even further, governments, in theory, have a strategic responsibility to improve the health of a nation and therefore have to work with voluntary and private groups to helps deliver objectives on this subject. Many governments around the world have also assumed the strategic responsibility to fund and support athletes competing for international honours.

In the last decade we have also seen the emergence of the private sector at a local level, whereby they provide opportunities to participate in sport at a cost. This will often be in direct competition with the public and voluntary sectors especially when it comes to the provision of health and fitness facilities.

So the trend now is for the boundaries between the three sectors to be more blurred. Funding of a sport service can often involve a mixture of the three sectors, with partnerships forming for the delivery of services. If we look closely enough we can see that the three sectors still retain their differences in philosophy, style and approach, although these too are becoming blurred. Today, we see a process which can be described as the collapsing of the sectors. This means that organisations from the different sectors are often having to work more closely with each other, or borrow some of their operating ethos and practices. At times we even see convergence of organisational goals and collaboration between two, sometimes three, sector organisations. Think for a moment about how your local swimming pool is run. Services traditionally provided by the local authority may well be operated by a private contractor for profit under licence from the authority. Consequently it's important that we establish what each sector stands for and how they continue to evolve.

PUBLIC SECTOR

The first of our three sectors is the public or state sector, which by its very nature includes local, regional and national agencies and government departments. These bodies will provide sport policy directives, offering funding to suppliers in sport and users of sport and, at a national level at least, support many specialist functions to supply elite sport, such as athlete development programmes. Governments will influence sport through national sports councils and associations, through lottery funds (where they are established) and through local authorities who operate on the front line.

Government has considerable involvement in sport. In Chapter 2, it was shown how, in the UK, in the early stages of industrialisation, government involvement with sport and leisure was primarily through regulation of private businesses. This was neatly summarised by Coalter (1990) as mortality (i.e. trying to improve people's health and reduce disease), morality (i.e. trying to improve people's behaviour) and social control (i.e. stopping riots and demonstrations). These are functions which are still relevant today, helping to explain why many governments become involved in sport. In many countries around the world, government involvement in sport has undoubtedly further expanded since the 1960s. As we saw earlier in Chapters 1 and 2, we can still point to some broad social objectives that include: health benefits (physical, psychological and social); community cohesion and social control (such as reducing crime, vandalism and anti-social behaviour). We can add to this list government involvement with the funding of excellence models and support of elite athletes.

Using a number of economic concepts helps give a further insight into why governments intervene to regulate sport, to help support, or even directly provide sport services, depending on the economic mix of the country. These concepts relate to:

- *Externalities:* when goods and services are produced, they can generate many positive or negative spin-off effects, which are not always factored into the price of the good. A classic example is pollution which occurs in manufacturing, with the cost of dealing with the pollution often being met by society. Sport is often cited as having many positive externalities or spin-off effects, such as improving health which can reduce the costs to health services. As shown in Chapter 1, it should also be recognised that some of the externalities can also be negative, such as treating sport injuries by health services.
- *Merit goods:* governments will often provide or subsidise goods and services because they are seen to offer many merits or benefits to people, which in turn is good for the economy and society: education, health, sport and leisure are classic examples of merit goods.
- *Market failures:* whilst the free market will supply merit goods for some, there are many in society who will not benefit as they do not have the money, even though it would be beneficial to the economy and society. In this situation a market will fail and the government is forced to intervene to ensure everyone has an opportunity to consume the

merit good. Education is a classic example of this process, but so too are many sport activities.

Governments have a very strong influence on the provision of sport at the local, regional and national level. It works in partnership with a number of providers to ensure that medals can be won and that people can participate. While its original motivation was to provide health, behavioral change and social control we have seen this develop over time into a broader recognition that sport can be good for society.

There is an economic argument too since the 1980s and 1990s that sport has also been seen as a catalyst for economic development, particularly in urban areas (another example of an externality). The main focus of this attention has been to redevelop and reimage towns and cities with a sport strategy which shifts attention from sectors that are failing in those areas. In Sheffield, for example, the collapse of the steel industry and manufacturing led to significant unemployment. Sheffield followed a sport regeneration strategy, linked to a major sporting event to try to rebrand the city and to stimulate economic growth. In many ways this was successful and has been replicated across the world. Cities have been revitalised through investment in infrastructure (take a look at what Barcelona did when they won the rights to host the 1992 Olympics) and facilities (take note of what London built for the 2012 Games) that would attract a growing service industry.

The economic importance and impact of sport is the focus for much recent research and points to the tangible, monetary benefit of hosting major events and sporting occasions which in theory may lead to increased investment and employment. Governments are often central to any activity that is sanctioned in such areas and are therefore critical in their success or failure.

However, as shown in Chapter 1, there are also potential problems. Many of the arguments outlined above portray a sector that is vital to economic growth and the supply of sport. Indeed the arguments follow a rather conventional and logical approach which is based on the values of a 'welfare state', though these ideas are not without their critics. A welfare state can cost significant sums of money, money that needs to be generated from somewhere and more often than not through taxation. Some argue that a 'government failure' model could be more progressive. Essentially this approach seeks to disprove the theory that governments can intervene in markets effectively or at minimum cost. The argument continues that the direct supply of government services and subsidies should be slowed to encourage the emergence of alternative provision.

In the UK, the government failure model has done a great deal to change and enhance the way in which public services are offered, including the provision of sport via partnerships with the private sector and even social enterprise models where communities run their own leisure facilities with lower government subsidy.

PRIVATE SECTOR

The private, or commercial, sector is now typically the largest sector of the three that we cover here, at least in terms of its monetary value. Since we entered the new millennium it has certainly been the most dynamic sector of the supply side of the market and the one that has seen the most growth. We've seen already that the sport industry generates substantial economic activity and a proportion of this is delivered by the commercial sector. As you would expect, alongside economic activity the commercial sector also generates many employment opportunities.

When we consider the commercial sector we need to think of it in two ways. First, by the activities and services that it supplies, for example, spectator events, commercial leisure clubs, business services, media operations and sponsorship. Second, by the size and scale of the organisations that produce sport goods through manufacturing and distribution.

Commercial organisations are generally concerned with one key objective – profit. It is through profits that they are able to grow and offer new products and services, satisfy shareholders, increase their value on various stock markets across the world, diversify their product and service range and even take over other companies. However, this simplification of the market i.e. that it is only interested in profit, can be a little misleading. Many commercial providers may simply use better commercial practices to achieve their objective. They can help generate efficiency improvements which save money, they target particular markets more effectively and they often improve quality. All of these approaches will make products and services more attractive.

The growth of the commercial sector over the last decade has been due to a number of factors, including the approaches to business outlined above. In reality there have been four main drivers to stimulate the growth: time, money, government regulation and technology. Briefly and in turn these are explained below.

- *Time:* in Chapter 7 you will see that time is a key determinant and constraint of demand. As people have felt more time-pressured (see Gratton and Taylor, 2000) they have less time for sport and only at particular times of the day. The commercial sector has been responsive to this and now provides 24-hour gyms, peak and off-peak membership categories, and specialist sessions for different groups of society, such as mother and toddlers, ageing populations or on-demand TV channels.
- *Money:* sport spending takes a significant slice of a person's disposable income and a large majority of spending now goes on sport goods and services. The commercial sector has identified differentiated products to cater for the variety of incomes people have, so that sport remains accessible to even those with the smallest disposable income.
- *Government regulation:* the blurring of the sectors is obvious here. The government will regulate, via policy, broadcasting and gambling markets. They may provide subsidies for TV channels and have even placed restrictions about the broadcasting of some sport events, such as the requirement placed on TV channels to share the broadcasting of the English FA Cup. Just think about how much commercial event management companies have to work with local authorities to stage mass-participation road races such as the Boston Marathon.

- *Technology:* unequivocally the development of technology has been driven in many ways by the commercial sector. The internet and mobile technology has changed the way that sport can be consumed, such as mobile TV, to online booking for exercise classes. With such a variety of technology-enhanced opportunities comes the capitalisation from the commercial sector.

We can see here that the opportunities for the commercial sector to be involved in sport are wide and varied. It's important to note the interrelationships here too. The provision of live spectating for example generates significant revenue across the world and each country will have their own favourites. Sports clothing, footwear and equipment is offered at various price points for many different sports, and manufactured and distributed across the world. The emerging importance of physical activity and health has led to a boom in private-sector health and fitness clubs which would traditionally have been supplied by local authorities at much lower price levels.

Commercial providers of facilities, services and products have had a significant impact on the use of leisure time and commercial companies and have to make good profits or go out of business. Whilst it has to maintain profitability, it is also starting to operate in a much more collaborative way with the public sector, in particular, to secure new and diverse ways of supplying sport. The commercial sector has and continues to capitalise on these opportunities by making efficiency gains and by improving quality and, most importantly, choice.

VOLUNTARY SECTOR

Just as the market fails to provide services which are deemed as worthwhile, which people can benefit from, so too can governments fail to provide. The idea of government failure gives an initial insight into why the voluntary or third sector arises. The voluntary sector is where the sports which are played and watched around the world began, as explained in Chapter 2. It is still an incredibly important sector in the provision of sport, with many people across the world referring to volunteers as the 'lifeblood' of their activities. Indeed a large proportion of sporting opportunities, from the recreational to the elite, is provided outside government and private sectors by people willing to give up their time for free. We hear stories regularly about the impact of volunteers (consider their importance of volunteers at the 2012 London Summer Olympics, the 2014 Winter Olympics in Sochi and the 2015 Rugby World Cup in England) and that events simply wouldn't exist without their time and dedication. There are millions of volunteers operating all across the globe in small sport organisations and local clubs, helping to provide structured training and competition for people of all ages and abilities.

We will often hear the voluntary sector referred to as the 'third sector' and it's important that we cover the rationale for this. Volunteers by definition give up their time for free to support activities. At a small local level this is clear to see when we consider the volunteers that stand at the end of a swimming lane timing young swimmers in an age-group gala. The third sector, though, includes voluntary organisations which are run by paid staff, not volunteers and traditionally these will be charitable organisations. Without these paid staff the charities would not be able to operate at the scale that they do. Without volunteers, though, these organisations would also fail.

Most sport organisations will be based around a voluntary club. These clubs and their national associations are also organised by volunteers and provide the backbone of the entire sport development structure. Even medal-winning elite athletes probably came from voluntary clubs when they started out. Some voluntary organisations are devoted to supplying sport on a continuing basis – local clubs and national associations are examples of these – but there will also be those voluntary organisations that exist only for the duration of a particular event or activity, for example, organisers of major events and the army of volunteers required to stage the event (though the organisers tend to be paid these days).

There has been little in the way of theoretical discussion of the role of the voluntary sector in sport. The Sport Industry Research Centre (SIRC) at Sheffield Hallam University, in conjunction with Sport England, has attempted to quantify the economic value of volunteers in sport in the UK, but this hasn't really been replicated elsewhere. In terms of hard theory, Gratton and Taylor (2000) point to the work of the economist Burton Weisbrod, who provided an economic rationale for the existence of the voluntary sector. Essentially he argued that two factors were particularly relevant to voluntary sector activity: governments themselves lack adequate information on consumer demand (at a local level at least); and government officials often follow their own personal objectives when making policy decisions. In this context the voluntary sector is vital as it will be in touch with local demand particularly where there are diverse demands. The voluntary sector can be a much more efficient provider and supplier of sport.

Despite its implicit independence, the voluntary sport sector is not without its critics and often has difficulty in supplying enough volunteers. Governments are often called upon to provide finance, advice and training which points to, yet again, the growing importance of partnerships and the blurring of the three-sector model. Governments have clear incentives to do this, not least that it is much more cost-effective to run clubs, events and programmes with a volunteering component. It also increases the amount of supply that is provided to the market.

Another problem of the sector may well be that the volunteers do not possess the skills or experience to adequately manage large projects or the up-to-date knowledge required to secure new funding opportunities. While this may be a criticism, it is important to note that as consumers we expect a level of management and, as such good, management is still valid in this sector.

THE BLURRING OF THE THREE SECTORS

As you've seen in previous sections, while we can define a three-sector supply model it is becoming increasingly difficult to draw any permanent lines between each of them. All three sectors are involved in the supply of sport provision and there are examples where partnerships emerge e.g. for the delivery of a major event whereby we see government funding, commercial sponsors and volunteer support, and examples where competition is apparent, such as the provision of health and fitness facilities.

Traditionally, according to Gratton and Taylor (2000), the commercial sector has been the dominant force in the spending associated with sporting excellence through expenditure on sponsorship, broadcasting and professional sport. By contrast, the voluntary and public sectors seem to play a larger role in the mass-participation markets. However, recent times have seen a period of increased government spending devoted to excellence (supporting athletes to win medals, for example) and more commercial activity in the mass participation market (24-hour gyms, for example). At the same time the voluntary sector is increasingly being professionalised with paid roles for traditional volunteer labour and with some voluntary clubs becoming more commercially focused operations.

It has become increasingly difficult to distinguish separate roles for the public sector and the commercial sector in the supply of sport and leisure opportunities. The number of public/private partnerships springing up to manage local sport facilities is increasing, alongside a steady rise in sport participation globally. Crompton (1998) has made an effort to provide some explanation for why this has been the case, pointing to an increasing number of new activities being available including aerobics, mountain biking, skating and beach volleyball. We can extend this to include the increase in road cycling, high-intensity interval training regimes, such as Insanity, and endurance events encouraging participants to push themselves to the limit by running through rivers, up mountains and over obstacle courses. These types of activities were not offered before and with no established supplier tradition the response has been an open playing field with all three sectors making gains.

Crompton also points to the reduced availability of public funds with agencies increasing prices for services and enhancing their product range by expanding into other revenue-generating activities previously considered the territory of private providers. In turn this has increased competition which has led to efficiency gains, differentiated pricing structures and new partnerships to maintain a level of service. With increasing prices the commercial sector has been able to offer more competitive programmes because of the greater opportunity for generating better investment returns.

SPORT AND THE GLOBAL MARKET PLACE

The concept of globalisation whilst widely used, is not always defined in precise terms, which leads to a number of controversies and paradoxes. The areas where there is some agreement in the literature relate to the idea of the compression of time and space, together with the increased interaction and interconnectedness of different people, societies and economies, for good and ill (Bayliss 1997, p. 7). The result is that the impact of events, ranging from natural disasters, acts of terrorism or economic collapses, travels far from the place of origin, reverberating around the world in a remarkably short space of time. Sport both reflects the process of globalisation and in turn helps to drive the globalisation process. What this means is that sport can show how the world is interconnected, such as the billions who watch the mega-events, such as the Olympics, or FIFA World Cup, often live, despite the different time zones. Furthermore, it also drives globalisation, such as the movement of people from around the world to attend sport events, or how fandom for teams and athletes can take root far beyond their original country of origin.

Sport, then, is a global phenomenon. This is further evidenced by the popularity of individual teams or major sporting events. Consequently it is appropriate that we talk about a global sport market. An increasing part of every country's sport market is international or global. Granted this 'part' may be small for some countries, but it is certainly growing. There are already sporting competitions that have a global attraction – over two-thirds of the world's population watch some part of the summer Olympic Games. Cumulative television audiences for the FIFA World Cup extend beyond 40 million people. These audiences provide opportunities for global sport businesses such as Nike, Li Ning or Adidas to target such events for their marketing campaigns.

Marketing campaigns that are part of major events extend beyond advertising slots and perimeter fencing. Companies sponsor individual athletes, teams and even training complexes with the intention of maximising sales revenue through their associations with sporting success. Moreover, the changes we have seen in broadcasting have been vital in accelerating the globalisation of the sport market. The English Premier League can be seen live in over 220 different countries thanks to the way that the Premier League has sold their TV rights packages. The most recent domestic TV rights deal, that runs for the 2016–2017, 2017–2018 and 2018–2019 seasons, is worth more than £5.16 billion.

The escalation in the price and value of TV broadcasting rights for major events has been the single biggest factor to affect the sport market. Coupled with the improvement in technology, the internet and mobile phones the world is a smaller place than ever before. Our needs and wants for live sport have been fulfilled and it doesn't matter (for the most part) where you live or work, you can still experience a variety of sporting choices.

The Football World Cup, the Superbowl, the Olympic Games and soccer leagues across Europe are just a handful of competitions that are extensively broadcast. The top eight television programmes in the USA are sport events. Over 130 million people across the world tune in to watch the Superbowl, making the advertising breaks the most expensive to buy in the world. Regular coverage of the NFL by Fox and the English Premier League by BSkyB in the UK have been critical in the achievement of economic success of these broadcasting companies.

This broadcasting power has led to changes in sporting competitions. Rugby league in England is now played as a 'summer' sport (although the season starts much before the weather improves), changing from its traditional 'winter' season in an attempt to improve the attractiveness of the game and to ensure that it didn't clash with other televised sports. The NFL is broadcast by BSkyB to attract a European audience and the Premier League is shown in, as mentioned above, over 220 different countries around the world.

CONCLUSION

This chapter has charted the development of the three-sector model and demonstrated how the public, private and voluntary sectors have begun to merge and blur their traditional boundaries. With all three now occupying space traditionally reserved for defined organisations it is easy to see how the sport industry has been able to grow so rapidly over the past 20–30 years.

As explored in earlier chapters, the sport market was historically led by the voluntary sector. During the 1960s and 1970s this shifted to a more government (public) focused model of provision with state intervention supporting activity through funding and policy decisions. However, by the start of the 1980s we have begun to witness the emergence of the commercial sector to a point that by the early 2000s the private sector became significant. The private sector has been part of the fastest rate of growth so that it is now the dominant sector of the sport market, making money up and down the pyramid (see Figure 6.1).

When it comes to managing sport, understanding how sport is supplied is important. The management of each sector that we have explored (public, private and voluntary) can vary significantly. Managing full-time staff effectively can be very different in the public and private sectors given the differences in the sector objectives. Managing volunteers presents its own unique set of problems, but managing in an industry that now engages all three sectors can be very difficult indeed. Some aspects of management though are very similar. All sectors need to satisfy their customers and achieve cost savings to ensure sustainability and provide value-for-money operations.

7

THE SPORT INDUSTRY AND THE BASIS OF DEMAND

INTRODUCTION

Our discussion here on the demand and motivation for sport is intimately related to the function of marketing which we explored earlier. In Chapter 4, we explained how the essence of marketing relates to understanding the needs and wants of customers. Just what is meant by needs and wants is discussed in more detail in this chapter, explaining why it is initially important for the sport manager to distinguish between a *need* for sport and a *want* for sport.

The chapter continues to explore the factors which motivate people to participate in sport, making a distinction between motivation and the demand for sport. A model which summarises these factors is presented towards the end of this chapter and has been designed to illustrate how a range of social, economic and psychological factors can shape the demand for sport, or act a barrier to participation. You can use this in management to reflect and consider what strategies could be adopted to sell services, whether this is for profit, or to achieve social objectives.

DEFINING MOTIVATION

In essence, motivation is about the factors which energise or push people to perform certain actions. In Chapter 3, motivation was explored in relation to what makes people want to work and, just as importantly, what makes them want to do a job well. Many of the underlying theories developed to understand work-related motivation are highly relevant here. There is encouragement for managers to try and better understand employee needs, so they can design working environments which better meet these needs, thus making employees happier and more productive.

In Figure 7.1 an overview is given of the variety of motivational theories which you may encounter in the different subject areas relating to sport. These are based around:

- motivation theories in relation to work;
- motivation theories in relation to sport participation; and
- motivation theories in relation to coaching and athlete performance.

Motivation in a work context	Motivation to participate, watch and buy products	Motivation in a coaching context
Questions: How do you get the right people? How do you get them to work? How do you get them to excel? **Examples of theories and writers:** Maslow's hierarchy of needs, Hertzberg's hygiene factors etc (see Chapter 3).	**Questions:** What do people want from the service? What makes for a good experience? **Examples of theories and writers:** Maslow's hierarchy of needs, arousal theories, etc.	**Questions:** How do you get children interested in sport? How do you sustain interest? How do you get people to train?How do you motivate athletes to perform at the highest level? **Examples of theories and writers:** Bandura's (1982) self-efficacy theory, Ames (1992) motivational climate theory.

Figure 7.1 An overview of motivational theories which may be encountered in different areas of sport

There are other areas where motivational theories can be encountered, such as in relation to tourism and adventure, but there simply isn't the scope to discuss them in this book.

Of course there are some important differences between motivation for work-based activities and sport participation, such as the compulsory nature of work, whether this relates to earning a living to help meet other basic needs, or having to comply with working day timeframes. However, in the context of this chapter, the primary focus is on exploring the motivation for people participating in sport.

Before these are explored in more depth, it is worthwhile getting you to think about some of the core underpinning themes which can be identified in these different theories, but which may use different terminology. For example, from the subject area of sport psychology and coaching, there are some very useful materials relating to athlete motivation to train and compete, such as Pelletier *et al.*'s (1995) review of motivational theories which look at athlete performance motivations based around:

- *Intrinsic motivations:* these relate to the activity itself, such as whether it is done for pleasure and satisfaction. These are sometimes classified around the three types of intrinsic motivations of: to know (pleasure and learning); accomplishments (surpass and improve); and experience stimulation (sensory and aesthetic pleasures).
- *Extrinsic motivations:* these relate to training or participating in a sport for other goals, such as being a means to the ends of gaining financial rewards, status or praise from the coach, or to avoid embarrassment, criticism or loss.

These notions of intrinsic and extrinsic needs are of interest for any sport manager, with consideration given to how other theories may deal with similar concepts, but simply use different terms and concepts. For example, Herzberg's work-related hygiene factors (discussed in Chapter 3), such as money, can easily be reframed around the idea of extrinsic motivators.

In the subsequent sections of this chapter, these notions of intrinsic and extrinsic needs are elaborated on, but focused on the sport consumer, identifying the key theories which help give an insight into what motivates people to participate and watch sport, or buy sport products. It is from this understanding that a manager can then design services which people need, want and so ultimately consume.

THE DIFFERENCE BETWEEN *NEEDS* AND *WANTS* FOR SPORT

A crucial starting point for understanding motivation is to consider how needs and wants act as the foundation for generating behaviour and actions. These relate to the key intrinsic motivating factors. In many marketing text books, the definition of marketing itself often focuses on the importance of understanding the *needs* and the *wants* of customers in order to design goods and services which are profitable. Simply put, it is about making goods and designing services which sell. The problem with these basic definitions for many sport organisations is that they are primarily focusing on *want satisfaction* for profit. Whilst this is fine for many commercial organisations, this focus may not be appropriate for many public and voluntary sport organisations with social objectives.

The claims made about sport as being something which is beneficial to individuals, communities and society means that a sharper distinction should be made between a *need* and a *want*. Whilst the two concepts are intimately related, they can also conflict, where at times the satisfaction of a want can in fact be detrimental to a human need. For example, if we think back to Maslow's hierarchy of needs discussed in Chapter 3, one of the first basic needs relate to physiological needs, such as the *need* for food and water, which must be satisfied in order for people to live. However, what people may *want* to satisfy this need to eat and drink can vary, and may involve buying food and drinks which may be unhealthy for them and contribute to poor health and disease. So in this instance, a need and a want may generate some points of conflict, which can also raise questions about ethics, even legality, about the extent organisations should always simply be about want creation and satisfaction.

So how does need and want differentiation work in relation to sport? Whilst for many commercial sport businesses, the desire for profit will mean they are much more driven by *want* satisfaction, for organisations in the public and voluntary sector; the focus could be more about *need* satisfaction, from both an individual and an organisational point of view. For example, sport programmes designed to get young people involved with sport may be faced with the tension of:

- children may *want* to get straight into playing competitive games, experience individual dominance and to try and win at all times;
- but what is *needed* is for a programme of activities whereby the children do some warm-up activities, skill development and team-building exercises, which they can then embed in the game, which meets the needs of the organisation in terms of developing future elite athletes, or the needs of the individual where they can develop skills which they can use throughout their lives.

HOW DOES SPORT MEET HUMAN NEEDS?

If we refer back to Maslow's hierarchy of needs highlighted in Chapter 3, it may not be initially obvious how watching or playing sport, or for that matter purchasing sport-related goods, actually meets human needs. Sport, in comparison with the basic physiological and security needs, may seem to be less important, whereby it only comes into play when people reach the top of the hierarchy in relation to self-actualisation, or a peak flow experience (i.e. a sense of personal fulfilment, satisfaction or contentment). Part of the problem is to do with the model itself and its simplistic, rigid categories, whereby one need must be satisfied, before the next one is progressed to. Whilst Maslow's model has been invaluable, helping to encapsulate the crucial idea that it is the desire to satisfy needs which generates human actions, it is, however, still too deterministic in terms of explaining human actions. It is therefore essential to add additional theories and concepts to this basic model in order get a deeper understanding about needs and motivation.

One way to develop this deeper analysis of needs is to consider how satisfying certain needs relate to maintaining a sense of health and wellbeing. It was explained in Chapter 1, how the World Health Organization define health as being 'a state of complete physical, mental and social well-being and not merely the absence of disease or infirmity' (WHO 2014). They are worthwhile reiterating as they can help frame social objectives. Using this health context we can see that sport can have the potential to fulfil:

- *physical health:* sport can help people stay physically active, which in turn can help them stay physically fit and well;
- *psychological health*: sport provides an opportunity for arousal, stimulation or emotional provocation, such as excitement, pride and happiness, which are vital elements in maintaining mental development and wellbeing, along with offering the potential for people to self-actualise (see Maslow's hierarchy of needs theory); and
- *social health:* sport can provide many opportunities to mix and share experiences with others, which can strengthen community identities, esteem and pride, all of which contribute to the human need of belonging.

It must be emphasised that sport has the potential to fulfil these needs, but the playing or watching of sport *does not* automatically deliver these benefits. As a reminder, we issued a caution about the simplistic, unquestioning acceptance of the beneficial impacts of sport in Chapter 1, whereby they only manifest themselves when the *levers* or mechanisms are put in place to help deliver the benefits. Indeed, when these levers are not put in place, it is easy to find many instances where the impacts of sport are marginal, non-existent or even detrimental to people's health and need fulfilment.

This importance of the concept of *leverage* cannot be stressed enough. It should remind you that the benefits of sport do not automatically accrue by the simple participation or staging of sport activities and events. They only occur when a manager puts in place measures, policies or strategies (i.e. the *levers* of change) to ensure the benefits materialise. By way of an example we can look toward the experience of gym membership; a person can attend a gym, use some equipment at very low intensity and believe that they are gaining some real health benefits however the true impact may be marginal. By contrast, exercise too hard and without structure and there is the potential for injury.

ELABORATING ON THE NEED FOR AROUSAL, STIMULATION AND EXCITEMENT

The hierarchical, deterministic nature of Maslow's model has perhaps been one of its key limitations: the idea that one set of needs must be satisfied before another need is moved to. Other theories and concepts are therefore needed to try to explain human needs and how they may shape sport motivations. Various theories relating to stimulation and play theories can be particularly helpful to give a more rounded understanding of human needs. Here it can be useful to think about the theory of arousal, which can be considered in two distinct ways, which are:

- *Arousal reduction:* this relates to classic economic theory of derived utility (see the next section), which also underpins Maslow's hierarchy, whereby the idea is that we feel arousal, such as feeling hungry, or fear, so we perform actions to reduce this arousal, such as eating, or seeking shelter and security. This can also work in other ways, such as how we sometimes use the term 'stress' at work, whereby if people have too much arousal they may do activities to help them reduce that arousal, such as having a drink, or going on a relaxing holiday.
- *Arousal increase:* more recent theories about human motivation have examined how people increasingly seek experiences which increase arousal, or are more stimulating. For example, for people wanting to climb Mount Everest, they are willing to take the risks of the physical dangers

that mountaineering in such extreme conditions entails. The desire to climb the mountain, which would no doubt be a peak optimal experience, may allow them to self-actualise, but would however entail compromising other needs, lower down the hierarchy, such as safety needs. It can also explain how emotional arousal, such as disgust, can override the hunger appetite, or how embarrassment can impede the sex drive.

So whilst we need food, water, shelter etc. to survive, what is also essential is a need for mental and physical stimulation if people are to have a life of quality. A simple way of representing this issue is to consider what can happen to caged animals in zoos. Whilst they are fed and protected from predators or other dangers, which fulfils certain basic needs, the lack of stimulation from overcoming challenges can mean quite simply that they are bored, which can mean that various psychological problems can develop, such as manic pacing or self-harming.

There are various writers and research papers which can give a further insight into the need for stimulation and emotional arousal. Tibor Scitovsky's various works helped give a more rounded view of human motivation for the consumption of goods and services, which critiqued the traditional, classic economic theory based on the theory of derived utility (for example Scitovsky 1990). This utility theory in essence argues that people buy goods and services because of the benefits (utility) that they gain (or derive) from their consumption. It is a model founded on the principle of rationality, where people will always choose the good or service where the most benefits are gained. What Scitovsky's work helped illustrate is that in reality there are many factors which can impede and distort rational behaviour, together with explaining how the old model of arousal reduction, could not adequately explain many types of consumption, such as, for example, the growth in dangerous sports, where what people are consciously seeking is an increase in arousal, not its reduction.

Csikzentmihalyi's work in 1992 gives further insights into the need for arousal and skill development. In essence, he developed a theory about motivation by focusing on the condition of human happiness and meaningful experiences. He noted that happiness is not the result of good fortune, or something that happens, but is the cognitive interpretation of events. The result was that he developed his theory of flow, which is an invaluable concept for sport managers to understand. Csikzentmihalyi (1992) argues that flow is a feeling and state of mind, which can have many similarities with Maslow's self-actualisation and peak experiences. It is something which is often hard to articulate, but intensely felt. The theory has been particularly useful for giving insights into why we participate in sport and adventure activities which have no extrinsic rewards, as they have the potential to deliver many moments of flow and peak experiences (Jackson and Csikzentmihalyi 1999).

Of particular value for the sport manager is the representation of flow theory, which is presented in Figure 7.2. At point *A* on the graph, someone who is doing a challenging activity, but does not have the skills, is likely to

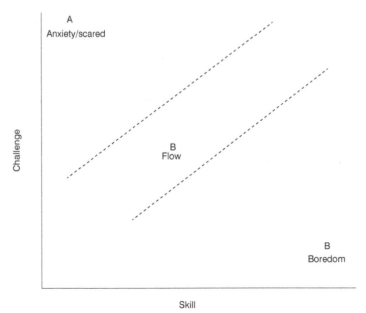

Figure 7.2 Graph illustrating the relationship of skills and challenges in creating flow experiences

feel uncomfortable, or even scared. This could be someone who has been given a difficult climb or abseil without ever having done the activity before; or it could be asking a young person to play in a football position, such as defence, without ever having played in a proper football game before; or it could even be an elderly person who is not very sport literate (see later discussion), who has never played a sport such as badminton before, and does not have the confidence to play. At point B, where the person is more skilled, but the level of challenge is too easy, then the person is most likely to be bored. Here, examples could relate to getting older children playing younger children at a sport, where they find it too easy and not very rewarding; or it could be the person who is doing a keep-fit class, whose level of fitness is much higher than other people's and cannot push themselves as much as they want. When the skills and challenges are in balance, at whatever level, this has the potential for flow experiences, which will give rewarding and satisfying experiences. This theory also begins to give an insight into the product life cycle discussed in Chapter 4.

THE GROWTH OF THE EXPERIENTIAL ECONOMY AND MULTI-LEVEL EMOTIONAL EXPERIENCES.

What these theories about arousal illustrate is that it is not a simple matter of arousal reduction or increase. It is possible for the sport manager to apply theoretical information about the design of goods and services to demonstrate how consumers can derive pleasure. This should, in turn, drive sales. Such theories about arousal and stimulation also give an insight into the growth of the experiential economy. Mintel, a key global market research business, said:

> In the developed world, the market for leisure, tourism and sport is becoming increasingly characterised by the seeking of activities which deliver heightened physical and mental experiences, which can offer more opportunities for personal development, and are of an excellent quality.
>
> (Mintel 2003)

These trends, Mintel (2003) argue, go to form the key components of the growing 'experiential economy' and have continued to grow since the report was first written. The term experiential economy (which should not be confused with experiential learning, which refers to the process of reflecting on and learning from experiences) was defined by Pine and Gilmore (1998) who observed the trend that consumers were seeking more intense experiences from both goods and services. The growth in adventure tourism and sports can be one of the more obvious manifestations of this, but it is important to appreciate that it does not just relate to elements of excitement and adrenalin. For example, one of the growth areas has been the demand for extreme luxury and relaxation, such as those offered on cruise ships, or short weekend breaks. Alternatively, it can relate to people choosing to do an international sport volunteering project, which focuses on education and personal development.

The link with the experiential and the seeking of flow experiences should be obvious. Traditionally, there can be the simplistic notion that when people have free time, or go on holiday, it is for relaxation, often encapsulated by doing very little, such as lying on a beach; the reality is that whilst some may choose this type of relaxation, they could also choose to do something more intense and challenging, either physically, mentally or both. As Csikzentmihalyi (1992, p. 6) observed, like all good adventures, they are not always pleasurable at the time, but immense satisfaction can be gained at the end, or with later reflection. This has some interesting applications in helping to explain the growth of various forms of amateur competitive racing events, or for the hardships which elite athletes must endure in order to compete at the top level, whereby it is not simply about the extrinsic rewards which can be gained by winning competitions.

These general trends in the experiential economy and experiential marketing are of critical importance for the sport manager to understand. It shows that customers are going to be more demanding, with higher expectations of a more intense or evocative experience delivered. In this regard sport has many advantages in its ability to deliver these heightened experiences and arousal, but they should not be taken for granted. If, for example, the competitive balance in a sport becomes so skewed, that the unpredictable nature of sport is reduced as one athlete or team always dominates, then boredom can set in and the experience reduced. It also gives a reminder that if other activities have the capacity to deliver more intense experiences, which can infuse other forms of non-sporting entertainment, then sport could lose out to them.

ROLE OF RISK IN MOTIVATION AND DECISION MAKING

The concept of risk has also been used to try and understand motivation and decision making. Ewart (1987) for example examined how the motivation to participate around certain adventure sports was framed around notions of risk and challenge. In one sense, using the concept of risk helps give more refinement to the theory of flow and the ideas of matching skills with challenge. Ewart argued that the seeking of risk is an important element in explaining why people participate in certain dangerous sports. This argument should however be given more refinement, as Cater (2004) argues that it is not necessarily the risk that motivates people, but the overcoming of the challenge and how it will make them feel. The risk is simply accepted as part of the challenge, which they feel confident in being able to deal with.

The idea of risk is influential in other ways, particularly how it can inhibit our behaviour. Fear, which can be inflated by the media (a process called media amplification) can be particular influential, whereby people may be deterred from doing activities not based on the likelihood of occurrence, but the severity of outcome. Examples of this can be found in news stories in the 1980s, where the fear of AIDS amplified by the media, created a great deal of misunderstanding, such as people refusing to swim because of they believed they were at risk of catching AIDS (which was unfounded). The point is that very often managers have to deal with these perceptions of risk which may be based on ignorance or misunderstanding, but which can have profound effects on participation.

TYPES OF DEMAND AND THE CONCEPT OF ELASTICITY

If needs give the starting point to understanding motivation, then when these individual needs are aggregated (totalled up), this creates a potential demand. Whilst demand is sometimes used interchangeably with the term motivation, it is important to maintain a distinction. It should also be appreciated that clusters of people who may share a similar motivation and desire for a sport service or product create a demand segment, which can be categorised in a variety of ways, which will be explained later. For now, it is useful to explain a few broad types of demand that are used in the discipline of economics and which a sport manager can find useful to know. These are:

- *expressed/revealed demand*: demand which is already evident and can be counted;
- *latent demand:* demand which is not yet realised, such as there being no sport services or products made available to customers;
- *diverted demand:* demand from one activity or facility, switches to a new one – this can be evident with gyms, where new facilities can be attractive for members and can often see people switching; sometimes it may be substituted for another activity, rather than just switching to another supplier of the same sport;
- *induced or generated demand:* demand for one product or service induces or creates new demands – this could be how a stadium can act as a catalyst to attract retail developments, or other even other sports, such as football pitches being used for rugby, and even, in the past, cricket;
- *joint demand:* this is important in sport, as many products and services need to combine in order to allow participation, such as hiring a tennis court, and having a tennis racquet and tennis balls.

Crucially, how effective price is in terms of regulating demand can depend on the *elasticity of demand.* In essence elasticity measures the responsive of demand to small changes in price of the good (price elasticity of demand – PED), or income (income elasticity of demand), or the prices of other goods (cross-price elasticity of demand). Demand is said to be price inelastic when a small price change takes place, demand remains the same; whilst demand is elastic when the price change actually creates a change in demand. In theory it can be represented by the following formula:

$$PED = \frac{\text{Percentage change in quantity demanded}}{\text{Percentage change in price}}$$

In practice, a manager may have a basic sense of the elasticity of demand based on observations and experience. For example, a sport facility offering keep-fit sessions for elderly, in attempt to increase usage, reduced the price by half, but which had no impact on demand. Demand, in this sense was inelastic. On closer investigation, it turned out that the issue was not one of price, but one of transport. In the end, the price was increased, with the additional revenue used to pay for a development officer to hire a bus and pick up the elderly people for the activity.

UNDERSTANDING FILTERS AND BARRIERS TO PARTICIPATION AND CONSUMPTION

Any sport manager should strive to understand what energises, motivates or pushes people to participate or watch sport, or purchase sport goods. This understanding should help managers design good-quality services and goods that deliver experiences, meet expectations and fulfil needs and wants. But it is only part of the process in terms of actually getting people to participate or purchase. The next critical set of factors which a manager needs to understand relates to:

- the extrinsic factors that can influence motivations;
- or the pull factors which can draw people to a product or service;
- or the removal of barriers which may prevent participation and consumption.

In the discipline of economics, these would be called the determinants of demand, but in this section, factors beyond those traditionally focused in economics will be considered.

Rodgers (1977) produced a very useful, but under-utilised model of social filters, which gave an excellent overview of the many factors that influence demand, such as age, income, education etc. The model gave an insight into how the potential demand is steadily filtered down into the actual expressed demand, or, if one uses marketing terminology, the segment. Rodger's many filters are reorganised into broader categories and presented in Figure 7.3.

In Figure 7.3, the model begins with the idea of needs on the left-hand side of the diagram, which provide the basis of motivation. Next, filters are organised around the broad categories of economic, social, physiological, psychological and supply factors, all of which are elaborated on in Table 7.1. To give an example of how it works, people who have young families are likely to find that they will have to adjust their lifestyles in comparison with when they were younger or a student. They may find that they have less time or money to participate in sports, or their involvement in sport may change, such as taking their young children to a sport club or training session, perhaps moving from active playing participant, to active volunteer supporter and developer. The other side of the model shows the management tools (discussed in later sections), which give an overview of some of the techniques managers can use to try and get people to participate, or remove barriers. Finally, it should be recognised that it is a dynamic model, where demand is never static, and people always have the potential to stop consuming, or switch to other activities.

The sport manager needs to reflect on how these different factors can shape demand for different segments. If the demand is not expressed, then this *latent demand* represents a *market gap*, which a new service, activity or product can be designed to fill.

The factors which may filter demand can also be viewed as potential barriers to participation, which can be particularly relevant when certain segments or target groups are focused on in order to achieve certain social objectives. An obvious

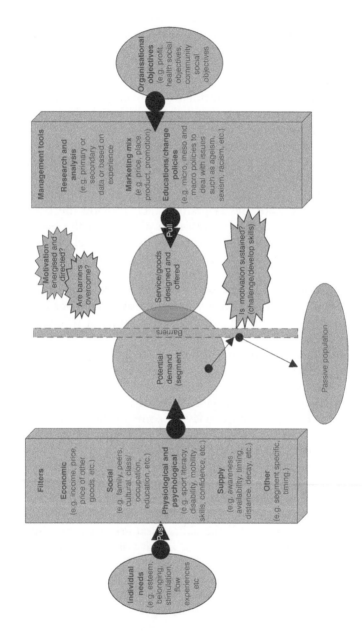

Figure 7.3 Adapting Rodgers' filter model

Table 7.1 Summary of key determinants, inhibitors, barriers and filters to participation

Category	Examples of filters or potential barriers
Economic	**Average cost of participation**: relates to fixed costs, such as expensive equipment, and the marginal cost, which is the cost of doing the activity; a sport like football, can be low on fixed costs and marginal costs which can partly explain its ubiquity in participation around the world, whilst sports such as sailing, may have expensive capital costs and marginal costs, such as launch fees. **Income:** the amount of disposable income for sport and leisure is important, but as incomes increase, demand may switch from one activity to another. **Prices of other goods:** this can relate to competitors, but it can also relate to how changes in prices, such as transport or fuel, can impact on demand. This relates to the idea that sport is a composite product and service. **Degree of substitutes:** can the sport activity and what is wanted be substituted with another sport or activity?
Social	**Family lifecycle:** as people move through the family lifecycle, such as having young children, they may find themselves both cash- and time-poor; but families in relation to sport are also a market niche; the experience for women can also be different from men. **Age:** in the past, simplistic assumptions were made that as you got older, people would participate less; this works to a point, but what needs to be considered is not that there may be less participation, but that it is of a different kind. **Gender differences:** females have different participation levels, often lower, which can be attributed to a variety of factors, ranging from family roles to prejudice. **Education:** types of school, private or public, or if a person went to university can be influential in the types of sport played and particularly the frequency that a sport is played. **Class:** this is becoming more complex, whereby the old terms of middle and working class, need to be broken down into more specific segments. **Cultural stereotyping:** this can take place at many levels, such as at the micro, which refers to individual perceptions and actions; the meso, which relates to the whole organisation or institution, such as a sport governing body attitude to a group of people; and the macro, which relates to the dominant views held by the whole society).

continued ...

Table 7.1 continued

Category	Examples of filters or potential barriers
Psychological and physiological factors	**Confidence and sports literacy:** relates to the familiarity and confidence people have with sport. **Physical ability:** can tie in with age and health. **Disability:** disability can be categorised in many different ways, ranging from locomotive dysfunction, sensory, cerebral or other dysfunction; the development of the Paralympic Games in both the London Olympics and the Glasgow Commonwealth Games illustrate how much para sports have come on. It is of interest that the London Olympics was the first Olympics where the branding and logo was the same for both games.
Role of risk	**Media amplification:** media amplification can create distorted perceptions of risk and inhibit people from participating. **Fear of outcomes:** people tend to base decisions on the basis of the severity of outcome, not always probability.
Supply factors	**Availability:** are facilities and services available? **Awareness:** are the opportunities communicated to people via marketing? Transport: how easy is it to get to the place? **Distance:** depending on the activity or its uniqueness, can affect the pattern of distance decay i.e. the further people have to travel, the more that the demand drops.

one can relate to income, whereby if people do not have sufficient income or the price for a good or service is deemed too high, then they will not be able to participate or purchase the good or service. In Box 7.1 an example is given in relation to stereotyping and stacking, to reveal how important it is to research and analyse the needs and potential barriers for certain segments or target group participation.

DEMAND AND SEGMENTATION

People can be divided up and categorised in many different ways, based on their age, interest, incomes and various other factors, whereby they may share certain characteristics which can allow them to be marketed to. This is the process of market segmentation and is of critical importance to sport organisations involved with both profit and social objectives. It allows a manager to identify groups of customers and design products

BOX 7.1 STEREOTYPING, RACISM AND THE PROBLEM OF STACKING AS A BARRIER TO PARTICIPATION

The issue of racism in sport is of critical importance at a number of levels. At the *macro* level (i.e. the national, societal level), in relation to the broad shifts in opinion and views held, racism is regarded as something which should not be tolerated. This of course does not mean that racism does not exist, rather that there is a broad consensus that it is wrong. When one looks at the *meso* level (which focuses on organisations and broad groups), such as the key institutions and governing bodies in sport, or at a *micro* level, such as the fans, coaches, teachers and managers, one can of course find instances of racism.

One of the potential problems is that of *stacking*: this is where an institution, coach, or teacher holds certain stereotypical attitudes to a group of people which influence both the types of sport they are encouraged (or simply told) to go into, or the positions played within those sports. It is often based on unscientific beliefs that the group possesses certain physical and mental attributes suitable for certain positions. For example Woodward (2004) examined the issue in relation to African Americans and the NFL, observing that black athletes tended to be steered for certain positions, whilst also making the more general point that apart from in a few sports, African Americans are still under-represented in senior management positions. More provocatively, Woodward challenged the myth that has developed that sport is one area in American society which has been the great equaliser. In the UK, Malcolm (1997) gives the example of how children of Asian background had a tendency to be steered towards batting in the game of cricket, whilst black children tended to be steered towards bowling. In Australia Hallinan *et al.* (1999) showed how the issue was relevant in terms of children and players of Aboriginal origin, whereby preconceived stereotypical attitudes would mean that they were perceived as having certain attributes suitable for some positions, but not for others.

Stacking can reinforce inequalities, particularly for certain groups being poorly represented in relation to positions of greater leadership and authority. To deal with this, managers can adopt a

continued ...

> continued ...
>
> variety of actions, ranging from those which target the micro level, such as removing staff or people who express racist views; some will be at a meso level, such as clubs being fined, or penalised, such as having to play closed stadium games, as has happened in some European soccer games as part of the Champions League; whilst some are more strategic in their development, such as more long term educational campaigns and the attempts to remove barriers to ensure that a better, equitable balance is maintained.

and services for them. There is no shortage of literature on the many ways that segmentation can be approached, whereby the different filters discussed in the previous section can help to organise different groups, such as:

- *consumers' state of being or demographics:* this can relate to health, age or where they are in terms of the lifecycle;
- *consumers' state of mind or psychographics:* this can relate to lifestyle behaviours, such as types of fans, leisure interests etc.;
- *occupation, education and income:* the occupation and education that people have can influence both their interests in sport and how they want to consume it.

A simple way to think of the issue is to consider the many ways you can be segmented for sport services, whether it is in terms of playing, watching, the type of sport, the teams you support, the level of participation or the products that you need to play. More examples are elaborated on in Box 7.2.

THE TOOLS OF MANAGEMENT

This final section considers how all these theoretical concepts can be woven together to produce management decisions in relation to designing programmes, services, products to meet needs and wants, together with considering how people can be 'pulled' towards a service, or barriers, which stop

BOX 7.2 SPORT SEGMENTATION

Sport England (2014b) have an interactive web site where a manager can use their geographic location, such as the postal code, town or city, to get a snap shot of the key sport users in the selected area. The data is based on user surveys which ask questions relating to participation and the frequency of usage (e.g. how many times they have been involved with a sport in the past week or month). In all they produce 19 different segments, identifying their population densities, some broad characteristics of the group and their potential motivations and interests. They also, very usefully, add some notes on the latent demand for sport. For example, three groups identified are:

- Sport team lads (Jaimies) are characterised as being around 20, white, likely to have finished or studying at a local college, living at home, with a likelihood to have a poor diet and lifestyle, such as smoking and drinking. They are most likely to be interested in football and use gym facilities.
- Stay at home mums (Alisons) are likely to be in their late 30s, with a couple of children, with their careers on hold. They are likely to be active in various school related voluntary work and projects. Interestingly, this group can have above average participation levels in sport, taking part predominantly in gym/fitness classes.
- Stretched single mums (Paulas) are likely to be in their early 30s, living in council or rented property with a number of children and be on state benefits. They are likely to have a poor lifestyle and diet, and experience feelings of stress, helping to justify a higher likelihood to drink and smoke. They are likely to be less active, with a lower participation in sports.

Whilst not perfect, this database provided by Sport England offers some invaluable secondary data to help managers design services, whether this is for profit or to achieve some broader social objectives.

Other countries have produced similar reports, such as the Australian Sports Commission (2013) report, but none, at the time of writing, are quite as interactive and detailed as the Sport England database. It has been one of the benefits of staging the Olympics where there was a desire to evidence the impacts of the games.

participation, removed. In essence these theories should be used to try to:

- *energise:* participants and volunteers must be motivated or energised to generate an action;
- *sustain:* after people have been energised, a manager must sustain that motivation to carry on purchasing or participating, which is where the concept of flow and the product life cycle can be so useful.

To paraphrase Torkildsen (2005), he stated that effectiveness of managers was about offering the right service, in the right place, at the right price, at the right time, which people know about. This gives a simple encapsulation of what the manager must do in order to get people motivated and participating in the sport service or purchase sport goods. This of course is more simply said than done. The discussion about filters and barriers is a reminder of the many actions, policies and strategies that may have to be put in place in order to create an opportunity for people to participate. The tools that a manager can use to deal with this issues are also represented in Figure 7.3 where they are summarised on the right of the diagram. In essence, the key tools which a manager can use relate to:

- *Research and analysis:* does the manager know what people need and want? This can be drawn from primary research (e.g. asking people directly via questionnaires), secondary data (e.g. using marketing data and reports already produced, such as those produced by Sport England), or simply based on their own experience. Understanding what people need from the activity, such as improving their health, spending time with the family, or receiving a stimulating, exciting experience is at the heart of being market-orientated, which is vital for offering profitable activities, or adapted to achieve social objectives (social marketing).
- *Application of the marketing mix:* aspects of this blend in with research, such as designing the right product, comparing

competitors' prices, developing appropriate communication strategies etc.

- *Designing quality services:* quality is often misunderstood as something expensive, but in fact it is about fitness for purpose. For example, a free weights or boxing gym, which pays little attention to the aesthetics or design of a building, can be a quality gym if it meets the needs of its clients in relation to being low-priced and offering challenging workouts.

- *Finance function:* all the activities must be properly costed, so a decision can be made whether to run a service to generate a profit, to break even, or if it is run as a loss leader (i.e. runs at a loss, but which helps achieve various social objectives).

- *Dealing with barriers:* these can be both operationally related, in that it may be a simple matter of trying to improve communications, the time of the activities or transport. In other instances, they may be more strategic, such as developing a cultural change in an organisation to deal with any prejudices or stereotypes. The strategic elements can also relate to create stronger market segments, such as targeting young people or schools to become more involved in a sport.

- *Sustaining motivation and participation:* here, the idea of developing people's skills and challenge is an important idea in terms of progression, and how the manager can stop people getting bored and dropping out of sport participation. Here, a critical element is the whole area of customer care.

CONCLUSIONS

What is being argued in this chapter is not that sport represents a human need, rather that stimulation, emotional arousal and challenges are needs which sport can at times help fulfil. It is an argument which mirrors Torkildsen's argument (2005) that there was not necessarily a need for leisure, but there are human needs, which leisure could sometimes satisfy. Of course, the degree to which sport can provide these needs will be determined by how effective the service delivery is and how people engage with it.

In order to fulfil the core marketing function of designing products and services which meet the needs and wants of the customers, this requires an understanding of needs and how they motivate or energise people. In order to make this analysis richer, a variety of theories and concepts can be drawn from the scientific disciplines of economics, psychology and sociology. These theories can then be woven into a variety of marketing models and processes in order to generate relevant products and services which help the organisation make a profit or achieve its social objectives.

EMPLOYMENT AND EMPLOYABILITY IN SPORT

INTRODUCTION

By now we hope that you can see the diversity and scale of the sport industry. We've covered all of the management basics to get you started, underpinned by a historical context to show how this unique industry has emerged and continues to grow. With this growth it's clear that the management opportunities available in the sport industry are varied, whereby you are most likely to enter at the operational or project level, moving towards the strategic level as your career develops. As the industry has grown, so too has the necessity for appropriate qualifications. A degree should now be considered as an important requirement to access the industry, along with a postgraduate qualification increasingly important if you want to work at a strategic level.

In this final chapter, these themes of employability, qualifications and entering employment are explored and explained. It begins by giving some initial context to the area. It then moves on to explain the key factors which help make you more employable in the sport industry. It then explains more about the nature of sport management degrees and how they are designed. Consequently we will move through this chapter to highlight the nature of employment in sport, how you can develop yourself and your career and then give you some pointers to help secure employment.

BACKGROUND CONTEXT FOR SPORT COURSES AND EMPLOYABILITY

The future health and viability of the sport industry will depend on a workforce with the correct skills, knowledge and appropriate training. There is an ongoing debate about how the current training provision, such as degree, master and continuing professional development (CPD) programmes matches the needs of the industry. It is a dynamic, ever-changing discussion, which reflects how the industry sector is constantly changing and being shaped by external forces.

Despite the diversity of the sport industry, it can still be considered as a discrete profession. For example, in the UK it enjoys chartered status, much like accountants, lawyers, doctors and so on. The Chartered Institute for the Management of Sport and Physical Activity (CIMSPA) sits at the top of the industry and makes efforts to bring together the variety of professions contained in the industry. We'll come back to CIMSPA later on.

For you there will be a requirement to study. Your pathway into the industry needs to be informed by sport courses and you will need to develop an awareness of personal development planning to enhance your own skills and attributes. You will hear the term 'employability' bandied around at regular intervals if you are studying already, or are considering study now; and you would be right to ask 'what on earth does employability actually mean?' In our view it's a fairly broad term. A term that is not always understood particularly well but, nonetheless, a term that you need to try and understand. For some it is skill-based, such as writing CVs, completing application forms, or improving performance at interview. For others, it may be about studying particular modules to say 'I've done employability modules at university'. For us, it's about much more than this.

Essentially there are two main approaches to employability, which are those that focus on an individual's characteristics and readiness to work, or those that will think much more broadly and expect employability to develop over time. This is exactly why CPD is so important. Yorke (2006) suggests we see employability in a holistic way, encompassing a range of factors that influence a person: getting a job; performing in job; moving between jobs; or improving their job. This is a crucial point. Studying is not the only answer. You need to do more than study, you need to gain experience, you need to network with those operating in the industry and you need to work out how your skills and experience match the requirements of work.

THE SPORT INDUSTRY AND A LANDSCAPE FOR GRADUATE EMPLOYMENT

Traditionally the sport industry has not been something for graduate employment. If you reflect back to the historical development of the industry discussed in Chapter 2, it should be clear why this was the case. Back in the 1950s and 1960s sport emerged from a technical requirement. What this means is that local authorities had begun to provide facilities which had to be maintained. Sport employment at this time, therefore, tended to be based around technical skills and jobs, such as pool and plant maintenance (e.g. ensuring the correct level of chlorine was in the swimming pool, how to operate boilers etc.). In the UK, the early professional bodies recognised this too and there were a good number of training courses available, some of which remain, in essence at least, with CIMSPA today.

In the UK, as the Sports Council became more centrally established and demand for sport and leisure increased, a more coordinated approach developed to improve the effectiveness of sport managers who ran facilities, or for those sport administrators who were beginning to provide some strategic direction for the industry. Moreover, as Minten and Foster (2009) point out, the reorganisation of local authorities and, in particular, their associated leisure services in the mid-1970s, enabled the expansion of sport in the public sector to appoint recreation managers to senior positions without any higher-level qualifications. Essentially, this created an industry where only a small number of employees possessed a degree. This was in part due to the rapid expansion of the sport market but also a lack of strategic vision on behalf of policy-makers and became a move that would haunt our industry for some time.

The acknowledgment of this training need and the requirement to get more qualified personnel into strategic positions eventually led to an increase in the number of sport-related degree programmes at universities, not only in the UK, but across the world. Indeed, the UK, USA and Australia for example, all have significant numbers of programmes and following the emergence of transnational education, they also have many partnerships in the Middle East, Far East, Africa and South America, leading to a the workforce becoming increasingly skilled.

There is now a growing realisation that there is an entry point for graduates of sport programmes, indicating a shift in the need to start at the bottom and work up. However, such a large-scale change takes time. There are still managers operating without qualifications who believe that new entrants should follow the same path. As the industry makes gains from a professional baseline we will see greater emphasis placed on graduate qualifications. Indeed, as you will see shortly, being involved in sport can produce some serious financial gains for people participating and working in the sector (see Box 8.1).

A key issue within the education and training provision for sport management is the employability of graduates, but in order to understand what influences access to employment we need to take a step back and consider two key points:

- *Concerns around over supply:* this is directly linked to the fact that sport- and leisure-related subjects are some of the fastest expanding and most popular disciplines in higher education. We've already covered why this is the case and you know that sport is now much more serious and less frivolous than it may have been viewed by some in the past.

Coupled with the expansion in the number of graduates entering the market it is also clear that sport has not always been seen as a graduate profession. Our challenge is to demonstrate the importance of degree programmes and putting this book together in many ways demonstrates how and why sport is so important and why it requires highly skilled leaders and managers.

• *Ensuring that graduate possess the right skills to enter the market:* we take this one step further though as we feel that it is vital that you can communicate and recognise your skills in order to be successful. You can learn all of the theoretical skills required to work in sport during a degree programme but if you can't articulate what those skills are, or demonstrate how and when to use them, you will not find a great job! In 1998, Hansen *et al.* provided some evidence to support this problem. A graduate's inability to articulate and provide evidence of the development of employability-related skills and attributes to employers leads to unsuccessful job applications. Many graduates saw their degree as a certificate without really considering its true value and how they had developed during their course. This in turn makes it very difficult to sell themselves to potential employers. The sport industry is moving and becoming more professional, you need to be ready for it.

THE CRITICAL ELEMENTS OF EMPLOYABILITY

We touched briefly on employability so far in this chapter and hopefully you are beginning to appreciate its perceived value, both for yourselves in terms of your own development, but also the requirements set out by potential employers. It's time to think a little more about the concept and what you can do to enhance your skills and attributes, in order to make you more attractive for an organisation to employ. In Figure 8.1 four key areas should be considered in relation to how they make someone employable in sport management, then how to continue to enhance your employability as your career develops.

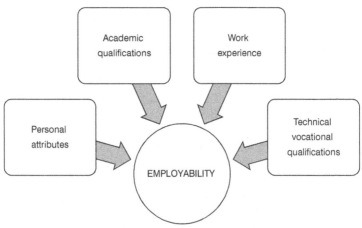

Figure 8.1 Key factors affecting employability

These factors involve the following things:

- *Work experience in general, or in a specific sport sector*: students setting out on their management careers can sometimes struggle to gain their first job because they do not have enough work experience. Here it can be just as useful gaining any managerial experience, as well as doing specific sport-related work. One of the real advantages of the sport sector is that it can offer many volunteering work opportunities which are invaluable for gaining experience, technical knowledge and networks.
- *Vocational/technical qualifications:* one of the things which can be so crucial in gaining initial work experience can relate to some quite specific technical qualifications, such as first aid or a coaching qualifications. Whilst this may not lead to a management position, it is invaluable in gaining operational work experience and may just help you get through the first paper sift when applying for work.
- *Academic qualifications:* there are many academic courses available, ranging from diplomas, degrees or postgraduate qualifications relating to sport, sport management, sport business, sport development, or many other variations. Sometimes, it may be the technical qualification which can

help with some areas of employment, but as your career develops, having a relevant degree can often be a critical requirement when applying for management jobs.

- *Personal attributes:* in terms of the previous areas these can all be gained in a college, university or work context. In terms of the personal attributes, the extent which they are already there or are developed is a much more complex area. Working with employers on project-based assessments or in a work experience situation will help you develop your personal skills and attributes. Don't forget to reflect on your performance and improve.

Don't forget that academic qualifications also offer you the opportunity to gain work experience. Many higher education courses will offer you the opportunity to choose an organisation on which to base your assessments, such as for a final-year research project or dissertation. Approach potential employers to see if they have any projects that you can base your academic work on. This may in turn give you an opportunity to demonstrate your skills and experience to the organisation (a type of shop window), creating an opportunity for employment. It may also increase your motivation to do a good job and make you externally accountable for the quality of your work. We have plenty of examples where this approach has created employment opportunities for our students and it costs you nothing but a little investment in time.

Many courses also offer a work experience or placement component to their qualifications; employers will place significant importance on completing meaningful work experience before they offer paid employment. Work experience will enable the application of your skills and attributes in a workplace setting and will provide you with the opportunity to develop specific vocational skills that are difficult to obtain during a taught degree programme (see below). When you return to your course, having completed your work experience or placement you can reflect on your experiences and begin to see the wider relevance of what you are studying.

Work experience can also, of course, extend to volunteering opportunities. Indeed, if you look below at the research that

BOX 8.1 **SPORT GRADUATES EARN MORE!**

In 2013, sports economists from Sheffield Hallam University have shown for the first time that graduates who participated in sport at university earn an average £5,824 (18 per cent) more per year than their non-sporting counterparts. The research, carried out by the university's Sport Industry Research Centre (SIRC), reveals that the current average salary of graduates who engaged with sport at university is £32,552, compared with £26,728 for those who did not.

The positive effects of sports participation go beyond earning power, according to the British Universities & Colleges Sport (BUCS) Impact of Sport on Graduate Employability study. More than half (51 per cent) of graduates say sporting involvement has helped them develop teamwork skills and leadership qualities in the workplace. The study finds that employers also recognise the benefits of sport in developing career-enhancing qualities, with more than nine in ten (94 per cent) of those questioned identifying a clear link between university sport participation and valuable skills and strengths in potential employees.

Furthermore, more than a quarter (27 per cent) of graduates who did not play sport at university have experienced a period of unemployment at some point in their career, compared with just over one in five (21 per cent) of those who did participate in sport. With 5,838 students and 112 of the UK's top blue-chip graduate employers taking part in the study – the results prove employers view involvement in sport outside of academic courses as a hugely beneficial addition to the skill-set for an individual's future value to their organisations.

Karen Rothery, chief executive of BUCS, commented:

> In a challenging economic climate, employers increasingly require candidates to demonstrate achievements beyond academic ability – key attributes such as team work, communication skills and leadership that can be developed through sport make a student stand out. The results of this research are proof positive that sport in higher education provides a recognised and valuable part of the student experience. Involvement in sport makes a real, measurable and positive impact not just on the student experience, but also on life beyond higher education.

And the positive impact of sport on a graduate's career prospects is not limited to participating and competing; sport also benefits those whose involvement spans coaching and refereeing, volunteering, being part of sports club committees and other support roles.

Professor Simon Shibli, director of SIRC at Sheffield Hallam and one of the lead researchers involved in the study, identified attributes of sporting involvement that enable candidates to demonstrate the personal qualities contributing to their employability, such as drive, ambition, motivation and leadership. He goes on to say:

> As the number of graduates increases, students need to do more than pass a degree to get their first job and to sustain their employability. The evidence indicates strongly that in the context of rising fees, engagement in sport is associated with providing a good career return on investment.

There is also significant evidence from employers that engagement in sport is a recognised strength and a source of differentiation between top quality and average graduates. However, it's not just about playing sport it's the involvement in volunteering and management aspects that can provide a competitive advantage in the jobs market.

Paul Szumilewicz, director of Retail Banking and Wealth Management at HSBC, graduated from the University of Birmingham in 2003 where he was team captain and secretary of the university's football club. He said:

> Playing sport at any level gives you a great university experience and employers really do view it as demonstrating personal and behavioural capabilities beyond your degree. ... A rounded candidate who shows commitment, academic skills and a wide range of interests is a hugely attractive prospect to an employer, and the attributes gained from participating and volunteering within sport are transferable across many industries.

Extract from SIRC 'Graduates who play more earn more', press release, available at www.shu.ac.uk/research/sirc/news/graduates-who-play-more-earn-more

the Sport Industry Research Centre did (Box 8.1) you will see that volunteering helps develop key skills and attributes for life in work. For many employers in the sport industry there is also an expectation that you will have volunteered at some point during a degree course, especially given that many employers operate in the third/voluntary sector (see Chapter 6).

UNDERSTANDING SPORT QUALIFICATIONS AND DEGREE COURSES

It is simply not possible to explain all the possible qualifications which you can obtain to help gain employment and develop your career. Indeed when selecting courses, there can seem to be overwhelming choice of sport-related courses. To help give an insight into various sport-based courses, which may explicitly focus on management, or have it as an implied or embedded element, a simply explanation of degree courses will be given.

As we have seen earlier, sport is a relatively new subject area which has been used for the basis of an academic qualification and has grown significantly over the past couple of decades. There are many different areas or ways which sport can be studied. For example sport can be studied in relation to the applied sciences of physical education or coaching, or it can be studied through the scientific disciplines of physiology, psychology, or sociology. To get a better understanding of the many sport degree courses that can be found, it can be worthwhile thinking how three broad areas are woven together to produce particular degree courses, presented in Figure 8.2.

In relation to the traditional scientific or academic disciplines, this refers to a particular area or branch of knowledge which can be studied and researched. It can be difficult to define exactly how many disciplines there are, but reflecting back to what was done at your school gives a broad indication of some of the most basic disciplines, such as mathematics, language, history, physics, biology and chemistry, with other disciplines, such as economics, politics or sociology also sometimes

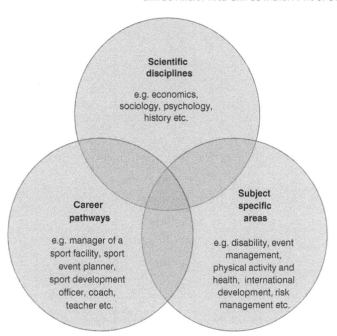

Figure 8.2   The degree mix governing the type of degree course

appearing. These many disciplines can be organised into two broad classifications of either being part of the social sciences (e.g. history, sociology etc.), or natural or pure sciences (e.g. biology, physics etc.). The type of classification can in turn have different implications in terms of how sport may be studied. Some sciences, such as psychology, or even economics, will vary as to which camp they can (or want) to be placed in.

The reason why it is worthwhile recognising these many disciplines and the broad scientific camps is that they can give an indication as to why, for example, a degree course may be classified as a bachelor of arts (BA), or a bachelor of science (BSc). In Table 8.1 an example of a range of sport-related courses are shown, together with which key academic sciences they draw on. Looking at this table, sport is not represented as discrete discipline, but as a subject area which is often studied in an multi-disciplinary way (i.e. the economics of sport, the

Table 8.1 Examples of degree courses and the key scientific disciplines they draw on

Examples of the scientific disciplines	Examples of sport related degree courses			
	Sport management	Sport science	Sport development	Sport studies
Economics	xx		x	x
Sociology	x		xx	xx
Physiology	x	xxx	x	x
Psychology	x	xxx	xx	x
History	x		x	x
Politics	x		xx	x
Applied science of PE	options may be available	x	x	x
Applied science of coaching	options may be available	x	x	x
Applied science of management	xxx		x	x

Note: 'x' quantity signifies the relevance of the discipline to the sport course.

history of sport etc. are used to examine and analyse sport) and, increasingly, in an intra-disciplinary way (i.e. specific areas of sport, such as the demand for sport, blend in theories drawn from economics, sociology, psychology, marketing, in order to try and better understand the nature of the problem and design better management solutions). An example of how these ideas of multi- and intra-disciplinary approaches work in practice is given in Box 8.2.

In terms of sport management and business-related courses, there tends to be a classification around part of the arts, rather than science. Indeed, although many management theories have attempted to use traditional scientific techniques, which can produce invaluable information, their application and the decisions managers take often come down to judgements rather than hard scientific facts. Looking back at Table 8.1 it should be clear that sport management courses often draw on the applied science of business management and economics. There are of course many variations, which can reflect the expertise and experience of the university, such as some places may have a stronger focus on the disciplines of politics or sociology rather than economics. It should also be observed how a sport-studies-type course's unique selling point is that they often take a 'pick and mix' approach, whereby they can draw on many disciplines, but where students sometimes begin to choose more modules related to a particular area. The final point to note is that there is an increase in sport-related courses which focus on more specific sports, such as football or cricket, or it may be in a particular area, such as sport event management, sport tourism or disability.

What will be important for you here is that you consider all of the options available to you and that you consider what your own strengths and weaknesses are when choosing a degree or master's programme. Consider the employability skills that you will be able to develop, along with how the course will enhance your own skill set, alongside an acceptance that a sport management programme needs to cover the basic functional areas of management covered in this text. The areas we have covered in this book are fundamental to any programme. Understanding finance, marketing,

BOX 8.2 THE IMPORTANCE OF MULTI-, INTER- AND INTRA-DISCIPLINARY APPROACHES IN SPORT MANAGEMENT

The importance of drawing different pieces of evidence from various scientific disciplines to help in management should be evident from the many discussions in the preceding chapters. To give another example, we can think back to what customers want and the sport experience discussed in Chapter 7. In that discussion, it showed how our understanding about what motivates people to work or to play sport has developed from people doing research in many different disciplines. For example, our understanding of how emotions work has developed from the scientific disciplines of physiology and neurology and the study of the autonomic nervous system. These works show how, in essence, our emotions relate to the chemical changes which take place in the body, but which we interpret depending on the context of the activity and the environment. These scientists have also discovered how chemicals, such as dopamine (i.e. the chemical in the brain which is related to reward) are released when we do certain activities, such as playing sport. All these theories can give some invaluable insights for the sport manager about the sport experience and how to design services that deliver a memorable and satisfying experience.

But it is not enough. How we interpret those chemical responses depends on the environmental conditions, such as the activity or events which are occurring and the degree of control that the person feels they have. Here the theory of flow can be helpful, which is drawn from the science of psychology. Furthermore, using other work, such as those involved with sociology, can give further insights into potential barriers to participation, or using economic theories to understand the influence of price. In short, in order to understand what people want, how you should design services to meet those needs, then how you can get them to consume the service, can mean many different theories and disciplines are used: in short, you are using them in an intra-disciplinary way.

human resource management and the ancillary management functions are vital to a career in the sport industry, so you need to cover them all.

To try and help you out here we've complied a list to help you in your decision-making process:

- Do I know what sort of career or area of sport I want to work in? (See Chapter 1 for the overview of options.)
- Are there opportunities to gain work experience on the course?
- Do students do additional volunteering projects outside of the course?
- Are there opportunities to gain additional vocational-related qualifications?
- Are there any areas of expertise and specialism which the university course has? (e.g. a particular sport, such as football, rugby, basketball, netball etc.; a specific area, such as finance, events, disability; academic staff who have published in certain areas; etc.)

CAREERS IN SPORT

All universities should now provide you with some useful resources and guidance to support your transition from education programme to employment though, rather surprisingly, students tend not to access these services as much as they should and it isn't until they graduate that they realise the importance of such initiatives. There are a number of things that you can consider before searching for employment, however, and applying some time and thought to these areas can help you to make effective career decisions. Arnold et al (2005) provide a useful framework here:

- *Knowledge of occupations:* find out about the area of work that you think you wish to enter. Your perceptions of a job or an industry may be quite some way from reality so it's important to dig into some of the detail. Working in professional football, for example, is often perceived as being well-paid and glamorous. The reality for most (unless you are on the field in an elite league) is that jobs are paid like most others and that hours can be long and unsociable.

- *Self-awareness:* we have touched on some of this already but it is vital that you can undertake an accurate appraisal of your own strengths and weaknesses, your real values and the things you really like and dislike. The more you reflect on your own appraisal the more accurate it will become. You will also need to be very honest with yourself to make this work.

- *Combine self-awareness with occupational knowledge:* this will help you identify the relevant career areas that you may be interested in. You can then explore these careers and choose the correct education programmes to access the job market and understand the continuing professional development needs that will be required.

- *Job searching:* the final step before you apply for anything. Your searches need to reflect your research and activity for the steps above. It also helps if these searches relate to matching your career and financial goals.

To help you with this we've developed an example to illustrate the composite nature of sport and some of the different areas of sport management roles that can be identified for a soccer club. Attention may initially be drawn to the footballer players themselves and the manager of the team. Just take a step back from here and consider how and who employs and trains staff? Who organises the fixtures? And who is responsible for the maintenance of the safety and quality of the stadium? Here there will be a variety of management roles including: managers working in human resources and personnel management; there are the people involved with marketing the games, designing posters, targeting groups and communicating deals and packages; there can be the managers involved with catering and retailing, in order to generate further revenue opportunities; and there can be the financial managers scrutinising income and expenditure. A number of clubs can also have a social enterprise or charitable strand to the organisation, where they are involved with working with key groups in the local community, such as in deprived areas, or people with disability. Branch out further and one can see the numerous enterprises and businesses which the club and matches provide. These can relate to the people actually involved with the manufacturing of football kits and souvenirs; it could be the tour operator who may put together packages for away fixtures, particularly fixtures which take place in other countries, such as the Union of European Football Associations (UEFA) Champions League; there can be the agents who support the players; there can be the charities who develop ties with the clubs to help raise awareness of their cause; there can be the agents who support the players; there is the media, ranging from news organisations and broadcasters involved with the sport; there can even be the public services, such as the police, who have specialists to deal with match-day security issues. All in all, lots of different positions to think about and integrate.

Why not take a look at some of the following websites to help reinforce our step-by-step approach to careers:

- global sports: www.globalsportsjobs.com
- leisure opportunities: www.leisureopportunities.co.uk

FUTURE CHALLENGES IN SPORT MANAGEMENT

Throughout this book we have made efforts to demonstrate the progression of the sport industry and point to a number of key future challenges that the sector is likely to face. Indeed, this chapter has extended the ideas concerning the management of sport and framed them in a context which is relevant to employment in sport. Hopefully, you have begun to think already about where the jobs are likely to be and in which countries they are likely to grow.

As a result of a smaller world economy (both in terms of monetary value and the recession that was experienced during the time of writing and the shrinking of borders with the advancement of technology) there are increasing opportunities to work in previously unexplored and less mature markets. Capital and financial investment will be easier to access as entrepreneurs and strong global organisations seek to maximise potential in emerging markets.

Technology also continues to break boundaries. Super-fast broadband has led to improvements in communications and can bring people closer together and the availability of digital TV and mobile telecommunications provides a canvass to market products and services to a worldwide audience. These new technologies also enable smaller companies to gain more control over the manufacturing and distribution of their own products and services making them more cost effective and increasing competition and choice in the marketplace.

As we have explored throughout this book, sport has the opportunity to play an important role in communities, whether these are local, regional, national or international. The local sport market has grown. Major sport teams now operate with a much larger catchment area than before and attract global audiences. Major events engage people from all walks of life and from across the social and economic spectrum. This places significant pressure on policy-makers to ensure that there is equity in the market. While the global sport marketplace may, on the face of it, appear to be dominated by the American way of doing business, the emergence of new powers, such as China, India, Dubai and Brazil, is changing the way products and services are offered and provide new opportunities for cultural engagement.

The key challenge for any future manager is to embrace this change. They must be able to provide innovative and cost-effective solutions in complex economic environments, embrace new technologies and understand older ones so that products and services can be provided effectively. These managers must be culturally sensitive and not only seek to introduce sport to new markets in the same way that it may have been introduced to theirs.

Reflecting back on many of the trends and issues discussed in number of key points may need to be considered by sport managers. These are:

- *Ethical management and leadership:* the issues of corporate social responsibility (CSR) and ethics have become more important. There is renewed importance of values, ethics and the leadership to be able to communicate them. These helps form and shape the culture and the operational ethos.

- *Creative, entrepreneurial managers:* Mintzberg (cited in Torkildsen 2005, p. 378) takes a different viewpoint from Drucker's (1995) observation that senior managers or chief executives are like the conductors of an orchestra; instead Mintzberg argues they need to be far more eclectic, thriving on problems, interruptions and constantly casting their eye over issues, problems and developments. In this sense, the chief executive is very much seen much more as the creative artist, who helps acts as a catalyst for creative innovation.

- *Traditional, hierarchical structures may change:* Handy's 1990 book *Inside Organisations* argues that organisations are more than structures and systems, and challenges some of the older, traditional hierarchical structures, preferring the shamrock shape to refer to the three different types of the workforce: the core workforce (what gives the organisation its uniqueness and experiences; the contractual fringe (people used to undertake specialist tasks, such as cleaning, catering, health care etc.); and the flexible labour force.

- *Joined-up thinking/inter-disciplinary/management function approach:* this can relate to the problems of bureaucracy and inflexible thinking. In government, we see the term joined-up thinking to refer to the need for smaller teams to work across departments. For example, at the 2012 Olympics, there was a need for different government departments, such as Department for Transport, Department for Education and the Department for Culture, Media and Sport, to work together to ensure that the strategic objectives of the event were met.

- *Change is a constant dynamic:* Peters (1987) *Thriving on chaos* and Pascale and Athos (1981) *The Art of Japanese Management…Why Were They More Successful…*

CONCLUSION

In this final chapter we have tried to raise your awareness to the importance of employability and education to help you access employment in the sport market. The challenges you face are broad and multifaceted, but with the right level of application and some careful consideration you have the opportunity to enter one of the most enjoyable and fast-paced employment markets in the world.

The future challenges for the modern-day sport manager are quite different to those experienced by early sport administrators. You need to possess a toolbox of skills and need to have an appreciation of the levels of management and how they interact with each other. The historical nature of employment in the sport industry does not make for easy access. The non-graduate traditions are frustrating but not insurmountable providing that you can understand and articulate your skills and experience.

If you wish to succeed you will need to be proactive. You need to network and generate opportunities for yourself and you need to capitalise on the partnerships and networks that the best educational providers will be able to support you with. Take advantage of opportunities to enhance your employability skills and undertake extracurricular activities such as internships and volunteering and identify your career goals at an early stage.

REFERENCES

Adair, J (1990) *Understanding motivation*. Guildford: Talbot Adair Press.

Adair J. and Reed. P (2003) *Not bosses but leaders,* third edition. London: Kogan Page.

Adams, J. S (1963) Towards an understanding of equity. *Journal of Abnormal and Social Psychology* 67(5): 422–36.

Alderfer, C.P. (1972) *Existence, relatedness, and growth: human needs in organizational setting*. New York: Free Press.

Ames, C. (1992) Achievement goals, motivational climate, and motivational processes. In G.C. Roberts (ed), *Motivation in sport and exercise*. Champaign, IL: Human Kinetics.

Arnold, J., Silvester, J., and Patterson, F. (2005) *Work psychology: understanding human behaviour in the workplace*, fourth edition. London: FT/Prentice Hall.

ASC (Australian Sports Commission) (2013) Market segmentation for sport participation, available at: www.ausport.gov.au/__data/assets/pdf_file/0004/523930/Market_Segmentation_Summary_Final.pdf, accessed 12 December 2014.

ASC (Australian Sports Commission) (2014) What is defined as sport? available at: http://ausport.gov.au/supporting/nso/asc_recognition, accessed 2 November 2014.

Bandura, A. (1982) Self-efficacy mechanism in human agency. *American Psychologist* 37(2): 122–147.

Bayliss, J. (1997) International security in the Post-Cold War era. In J. Bayliss and S. Smith (eds), *The globalization of world politics: an introduction to international relations*. Oxford: Oxford University Press.

BBC (2014) US athletes use crowdfunding to support Olympic dream, available at: www.bbc.co.uk/news/magazine-26166343, accessed 12 December 2014.

BBC Sport (2011) Sepp Blatter's most famous gaffes, available at: www.bbc.co.uk/sport/0/football/15781405, accessed 20 December 2014.

Beech, J. and Chadwick, S. (eds) (2004) *The business of sport management*. London: Prentice Hall.

Biddle, S. and Mutrie, N. (2008) *Psychology of physical activity: determinants, well-being & interventions,* second edition. London: Routledge.

Blake, R. R. and Mouton, J.S. (1981) *The new managerial grid*, fourth edition. Houston, TX: Gulf Publishing.

Braithwaite, T. W. (2004) Human resource management in sport. In Beech, J. and Chadwick, S. (eds), *The business of sport management.* London: Prentice Hall.

Burke, R. (1999) *Project management: planning and control*, third edition. Chichester: Wiley.

Campbell, D. (2004) I can take you to Olympic gold, *The Observer*, 22 February, available at: www.theguardian.com/sport/2004/feb/22/rugbyunion.deniscampbell, accessed 22 April 2015.

Carr, E.H. (1961) *What is history.* London: Penguin.

Cater, I. (2004) Playing with risk? Participant perceptions of risk and management implications in adventure tourism. *Tourism Management*, 27(2): 316–325.

CIM (2009) Marketing and the 7Ps: a brief summary of marketing and how it works, available at: www.cim.co.uk/files/7ps.pdf, accessed 15 April 2015.

Clarke, J, and Critcher, C (1988) *The devil makes work: leisure in capitalist Britain*. Urbana: University of Illinois Press.

Coalter, F. (1990) The mixed economy: the historical background to the development of the commercial, voluntary and public sectors of the leisure industries. In I. Henry (ed.), *Management and planning in the leisure industries*. London: Macmillan.

Coalter, F. (2013) *Sport for development: what game are we playing*. London: Routledge.

Collins, T. (2013) *Sport in capitalist society*. London: Routledge.

Council of Europe (2001) European Sports Charter (revised edition), available at: www.coe.int/t/dg4/epas/resources/charter_en.asp, accessed 2 November 2014.

Crabbe, T. and Wagg, S. (2000) A carnival of cricket? The cricket world cup, 'race' and the politics of the carnival. *Sport and Society*, (3)2: 70-88.

Critcher, C. (1982) Football since the war, in B. Waites, T. Bennett and G. Martin (eds) *Popular culture: past and present*. London Croom Helm.

Croke, C. and Harper, M. (2011) The rise of the baggy green as an Australian symbol: the modern invention of an age-old tradition. *Sport in Society*, 14(5): 685–700.

Crompton, J. (1998) Emergence of the unfair competition issue in United States recreation. *Managing Leisure*. 1(4): 199–212.

Csikzentmihalyi, M. (1992) *Flow: the psychology of optimal experiences*. London: Harper Collins Publishers.

DoE (Department of Environment) (1975) Parliamentary white paper 'Sport and Recreation'. London: HMSO.

Drucker, P.F. (1995) *People and performance: the best of Peter Drucker on management*. London: Routledge.

Ewart, A. (1987) Recreation in the outdoor setting: a focus on adventure-based recreational experiences. *Leisure Information Quarterly*. 14(1): 5–7.

Fayol, H. (1916 [2013]) *General and industrial management*. Eastford, CT: Martino Fine Books.

Follett, M.P. (1918 [2014]) *The new state: Group organization the solution of popular government*. Whitefish, MT: Literary Licensing, LLC.

FIFA (2006) FIFA's fight against child labour, available at: www.fifa.com/aboutfifa/socialresponsibility/news/newsid=102476/, accessed 2 November 2014.

Gemmell, J. (2011): 'The Springboks were not a Test side': the foundation of the Imperial Cricket Conference. *Sport in society: cultures, Commerce, Media, Politics* 14(5): 701–718.

Goleman, D. (2000) Leadership that gets results. *Harvard Business Review*, available at: https://hbr.org/2000/03/leadership-that-gets-results/ar/1, accessed 20 October 2014.

Governance Hub and Cooperatives UK (2009) Governance and organisational structures, available at: www.socialenterpriseworks.org/wp-content/uploads/2009/05/governance_and_organisational_structures.pdf, accessed 12 September 2014.

Gratton, C. and Taylor, P. (2000) *Economics of sport and recreation*. London: Routledge.

Hallinan, C., Bruce, T and Harper, M. (1999) Up front and beyond the centre line: Australian aborigines in elite Australian rules football. *International Review for the Sociology of Sport*. 34(4): 369–383.

Handy, C. B. (1985) *Understanding organisations*, third edition. Harmondsworth: Penguin Books.

Hansen, A., Minten, S. and Taylor, P. (1998) Graduate recruitment and development in the sport and leisure industry. DfEE/SPRITO/UK Standing Conference for Leisure, Recreation and Sport.

Heizer, J. and Render, B. (2004) *Operational management*, seventh edition. London: Pearson.

Henry, I. (1993) *The politics of leisure policy*. London: CABI.

Hobsbawm, E. and Ranger, T. (eds). (2012) *The invention of tradition*. Cambridge: Cambridge University Press.

Horne, J., Tomlinson, A., Whannel, G. and Woodward, K. (2013) *Understanding sport: a socio-cultural analysis*. London: Routledge.

Hoye, R., Smith, C. T., Nicholson, M., Stewart, B. and Westerbeek, H. (2012) *Sport management, principles and applications*. New York: Routledge.

Jackson, S. A. and Csikszentmihalyi, M. (1999) *Flow in sports: the keys to optimal experiences and performances*. Champaign, IL: Human Kinetics.

James, C.L.R. (1963) *Beyond a boundary*. London: Hutchinson.

Johnson, G., Scholes, K. and Whittington, R. (2008) *Exploring corporate strategy*. London: Pearson Education.

Katz, D. and Kahn, R.L. (1978) *The social psychology of organizations*. New York: Wiley.

Kotler, P. (1988) *Marketing management*, sixth edition. Englewood Cliffs, NY: Prentice Hall.

Lee, D. (2015) Tennis racquet technology comes with strings attached, BBC News, 13 January, available at: www.bbc.co.uk/news/business-30746221, accessed 14 January 2015.

Likert, R. (1967) *The human organisation: its management and value*. New York: McGraw-Hill.

Liu, J., Srivasta, A., and Woo, H.S. (1998) Transference of skills between sports and business. *Journal of European Industrial Training*, 22(3): 93–112.

Malcom, D. (1997) Stacking in cricket: a figurational sociological reappraisal of centrality. *Sociology of Sport Journal*, 14(3): 263–282.

Mallon, B. and Buchanan, I (2006). Historical dictionary of the Olympic Movement. Lanham, MD: Scarecrow Press.

Maslow, A. H. (1943) A theory of human motivation. *Psychological Review* 50(4): 370–396.

Masteralixis, P., Barr, C. A. and Hums, M. A. (2005) *Principles and practice of sport management*, second edition. London: Jones & Bartlett Publishers.

McGregor, D. (1960) *The human side of enterprise*. New York: McGraw-Hill.

McMahon-Beattie, U. and Yeoman, I. (2004) *Sport and leisure operations management*. London: Thomson.

Mintel (2003) *Alternative destinations for the future*, Mintel Group.

Minten, S., and Foster, W. (2009) Human resource management. In K. Bill (ed.), *Sport management*. Exeter: Learning Matters.

Mintzberg, H. (1989) *Mintzberg on management: inside our strange world of organizations*. New York: Simon and Schuster.

Nair, N. (2011) Cricket obsession in India: through the lens of identity theory. *Sport in Society*, 14(5): 569–580.

Nicholas J.M. (2001) *Project management for business and technology: principles and practice*. London: Prentice Hall.

Nike (2010) Nike, Inc. introduces 2015 global growth strategy, available at: http://news.nike.com/news/nike-inc-introduces-2015-global-growth-strategy, accessed 15 April 2015.

Nike (2014) The official board, available at: www.theofficialboard.com/org-chart/nike, accessed 22 November 2014.

O'Conell, F. (1996) *How to run successful projects II*. London: Prentice Hall.

Pelletier, L.G., Fortier, M.S., Vallerand, R.J.,Tuson, K. M., Briere, N. M. and Blais, M.R. (1995) Towards a new measurement of intrinsic motivation, extrinsic motivation, and amotivation in sports: the Sport Motivation Scale (SMS). *Journal of Sport and Exercise Psychology*, 17, 35–53

Peter, L. (1986) *The Peter pyramid*. London: Allen and Unwin.

Peters, H. (1996) Peer coaching for executives. *Training and Development*, 50(3): 39–41.

Pine, B. J. and Gilmore, J. H. (1998) *The experience economy: work is a theatre and every business a stage*. Boston, MA: Harvard Business School Press.

Roberts, K. (2004) *The leisure industry*. London: Palgrave.

Robbins, S. and Judge, T. (2012) *Organisational behaviour*, 15th edition. Cambridge: Pearson.

Rodgers, B. (1977), *Rationalizing sports policies, sport in its social context: international comparisons*. Strasbourg: Council of Europe.

RowZ. (2014) The end of growth: have English football attendances peaked and what happens next? available at: http://rowzfootball.wordpress.com/2012/11/14/the-end-of-growth-have-english-football-attendances-peaked-and-what-happens-next/, accessed 12 December 2014.

Scitovsky, T. (1990) The benefits of asymmetric markets. *The Journal of Economic Perspectives* 4(1): 135–148.

Sport England (2014a). What is sport, available at: www.sportengland.org/our-work/national-work/national-governing-bodies/sports-that-we-recognise/, accessed 12 November 2014.

Sport England (2014b). Market segmentation, available at: http://segments.sportengland.org, accessed 18 December 2014.

Stewart, B. (2014) *Sport funding and finance*, second edition. London: Routledge.

Sydney University Sport and Fitness (2014) Organisational chart, available at: www.susf.com.au/page/organisational_chart.html, accessed 22 November 2014.

Tannenbaum, A.S. and Schmit, W.H. (1958) How to choose a leadership pattern. *Harvard Business Review* 36: 95–101.

Taylor, F.W. (1911) *The principles of scientific management.* New York and London: Harper Brothers.

Taylor, P. (ed.) (2012) *Torkildsen's sport and leisure management.* London: Taylor and Francis.

Torkildsen, G. (2005) *Sport and leisure management,* fifth edition London: Taylor and Francis.

UN (2005) *Sport as a tool for development and peace: towards achieving the United Nations millennium development goals.* Report from the UN Inter-agency task force on sport for development and peace, available at: www.un.org/sport2005/resources/task_force.pdf, accessed 24 November 2014.

Vroom, V.H. (1964) *Work and motivation.* San Francisco, CA: Jossey-Bass.

Wagner, H.L. (1964) Displacement of scope: a problem of the relationship between small-scale and large-scale sociological theories, *The American Journal of Sociology,* 69(6): 571–584.

Watt, D.C. (1998) *Event management in leisure and tourism.* Harlow: Addison Wesley Longman.

Weese, W. (1996) Follow the leader, *Recreation,* December, 26–30.

WHO (2014) WHO definition of health, available at: www.who.int/about/definition/en/print.html, accessed 12 November 2014.

Wilson, R. (2011) *Managing sport finance.* London: Routledge.

Wolfenden Committee (1960) *Sport and the community.* London: CCPR.

Woodward, J. R. (2004) Professional football scouts: an investigation of racial stacking. *Sociology of Sport Journal,* 21(4): 356–375.

Woodward, C. (2005) *Winning!* London: Hodder Paperbacks.

Wolsey, C (2011) Management skills and techniques, in P. Taylor and G. Torkildsen (eds), *Torkildsen's sport and leisure management,* London: Taylor and Francis Ltd.

Yorke, M. (2006) *Employability in higher education: what is it – what it is – what it is not.* York: Higher Education Academy.

INDEX